# THE GRUNDRISSE

*the text of this book is printed on 100% recycled paper*

*Books by David McLellan*

THE GRUNDRISSE
MARX BEFORE MARXISM

# THE GRUNDRISSE

## KARL MARX

*Edited and translated by*
DAVID McLELLAN

HARPER TORCHBOOKS
Harper & Row, Publishers
New York • Evanston • San Francisco • London

A hardcover edition of this book is available from Harper & Row Publishers, Inc.

First HARPER TORCHBOOK edition published 1972.

STANDARD BOOK NUMBER: 06–131663–6

TO
STEPHANIE

# Contents

# Preface

I⊤ is indicative of the deficiencies of much current discussion about Marx that the *Grundrisse*, which – as I argue here in my Introduction – is the centrepiece of his work, should yet be the last of his major writings to be translated into English. The present edition is by no means a full-scale scholarly one and has the modest aim of making available the most important passages of this vital text with enough commentary to make them intelligible in the context of Marx's thought as a whole. Since this is the first translation and the text is in places very difficult, I have tried to follow the original as closely as possible for fear of over-interpretation. At the same time, I have tried to make the text readable: I have added paragraphs and cut down Marx's italicising drastically. The titles of the sections are my own and I have added a small introductory comment to each to give the reader an idea of Marx's general line of argument. I am grateful to Brian Barefoot for working on the first draft of the translations; also to my colleagues Christine Marsh and Derek Allcorn for their valuable advice.

D. M.

*Littlecroft,*
*Chilham,*
*Kent*
*June 1970*

# THE GRUNDRISSE

# Introduction

DURING the century or so since Marx's thought has been the object of widespread attention and comment, views as to what constitutes the kernel of his doctrine have been widely different. Until well on in this century, Marx was viewed as an economist, the author of *Capital*, who had claimed, by his analysis of the contradictions of capitalist society, to have demonstrated its inevitable collapse. This emphasis was the product both of the intellectual climate at the end of the nineteenth century and of the nature of those of Marx's writings that were then available to the public. By the 1920s, however, interest in Hegel had revived, Lukacs and Korsch had given novel interpretations of Marx in the light of this revival, and, above all, around 1930 the publication of Marx's early writings – doctoral thesis, 'Critique of Hegel's Philosophy of the State' and particularly the *Paris Manuscripts* – caused a remarkable change of emphasis. Wide discussion of the early writings was only possible after the war and the first English version of the *Paris Manuscripts* was not produced until the very end of the 1950s. This reappraisal may have been slow, but, in the minds of some, it was radical, and Marx was discovered to be really a humanist, an existentialist, even a 'spiritual existentialist'.[1] This obviously raised the problem of the relationship of Marx's earlier to his later writings: was there one Marx or two? Schools formed: possibly the largest number maintained that the young Marx was richer than the old Marx, who had lost much of his original humanist vision;[2] others maintained that the fundamental inspiration of Marx's thought was indeed to be found in the *Paris Manuscripts*, but that Marx's

[1] E. Fromm, *Marx's Concept of Man* (New York, 1961) p. 5.
[2] These are particularly well represented in Germany, following the interpretation given by Landshut and Mayer in their introduction to Marx's *Frühschriften* (Stuttgart, 1932). Perhaps the best example is H. Popitz, *Der entfremdete Mensch* (Basel, 1953).

later writings were a development of this inspiration,[1] still others, mostly orthodox communists, claimed that the *Paris Manuscripts* were a transitory stage in Marx's development and rendered superfluous by later works.[2] The latest suggestion has been that Marx should be divided into four: 1840–44, early works; 1845, works of transition; 1845–57, works of maturation; and 1857–83, works of maturity.[3]

This debate tends to be useless in the same way that the pre-1930 interpretations of Marx do. Just as those interpretations could not take into account the bulk of Marx's early writings and thus are necessarily deficient, so the interpretations mentioned above are equally deficient in that they neglect what is, in a sense, the most fundamental of all Marx's writings – the *Grundrisse der Kritik der politischen Ökonomie.*[4] The first public mention of this thousand-page manuscript (apparently unknown to Engels) was made by David Rjazanow, the director of the Marx-Engels Institute in Moscow, who announced its discovery to the Socialist Academy in Moscow in 1923. The German translation of this communication is published in *Archiv für die Geschichte des Sozialismus und der Arbeiterbewegung,* volume 11 (1925). It was originally intended to publish the *Grundrisse* in the *MEGA* edition, begun in 1927, which contains the early writings. *MEGA* was, however, discontinued and the *Grundrisse* was eventually

[1] This interpretation is most popular in France, and a good example would be J. Y. Calvez, *La Pensée de Karl Marx* (Paris, 1956); or Fromm's book quoted above.

[2] For example E. Bottigelli, *La Genèse du socialisme scientifique* (Paris, 1967).

[3] L. Althusser, *For Marx* (London, 1970) p. 27. This book, which may well be profound but is certainly obscure, discusses at great length the question of whether it is possible to periodise Marx's thought, and the importance, for deciding this question, of the influence of Hegel on Marx. However, Althusser never once even mentions the *Grundrisse* in this context! For all his playing down of Hegel's influence on Marx, Althusser's approach has a certain resemblance to Hegel – and not only in convolution of style: Althusser's 'structure' functions much as Hegel's 'idea' – an independent entity determining the very items from which it has arisen.

[4] It should be noted that this title is not Marx's but stems from the first editors of his manuscripts. It could be misleading in that *Critique of Political Economy* was the subtitle of *Capital,* and, as I show later, the *Grundrisse* is much more than a rough draft of *Capital.*

published in a separate edition in Moscow in 1939 with a supplementary volume in 1941. The time and place of its publication precluded any serious attention being paid to it. Only in 1953, when Dietz Verlag produced a single-volume edition, did the *Grundrisse* become available in the West. There is still no English translation.[1] It is, however, the centrepiece of Marx's thought: any selection of Marx's writings that does not quote fairly widely from the *Grundrisse* must be judged severely inadequate;[2] and any discussion of the continuity of Marx's thought that does not take account of the *Grundrisse* would be doomed from the start. In the understanding of Marx, history has indeed repeated itself and the evaluations that exegetes of Marx applied to the *Manuscripts* – 'The revelation of authentic Marxism. . . . The central work of Marx, the crucial stage in the development of his thought',[3] etc. – sound much more plausible when applied to the *Grundrisse*.

Marx's correspondence (and to some extent his published work) is littered with plans and projects for publication. The first is to be found in the preface that he sketched out to the *Paris Manuscripts*. Here he stated that

> . . . I shall, therefore, publish my critique of law, morals, politics, etc. in a number of independent brochures; and finally I shall endeavour, in a separate work, to present the interconnected whole, to show the relationships between the parts, and to provide a critique of the speculative treatment of this material. That is why, in the present work, the relationships of political economy with the state, law, morals, civil life, etc., are

[1] Marcuse is one of the few authors to have quoted extensively from the *Grundrisse*, whose importance was first emphasised in English by Martin Nicolaus, 'The Unknown Marx', *New Left Review* (1968). A full translation of the text will be published in the English edition of the works of Marx and Engels, but this will not be available for several years. There is a good English translation of the self-contained section on *Precapitalist Economic Formations* with an excellent introduction by E. J. Hobsbawm (London, 1964). The French translation of the whole work which has recently been published (Paris, 1967–1968), is untrue to the original by wishing systematically to exclude or minimise the Hegelian cast of Marx's work.

[2] Every selection known to me – including that of Bottomore and Rubel, which is in many ways the best – must be so judged.

[3] K. Marx, *Die Frühschriften*, ed. Landshut and Mayer, p. xiii.

touched upon only to the extent that political economy itself expressly deals with these subjects.[1]

In the event, of course, Marx was to spend a whole lifetime on this 'first brochure'. In January 1845 Marx signed a contract with Leske, a Darmstadt publisher, for a *Critique of Politics and Economics*. Engels wrote to Marx: 'make sure that you get your book on economics finished even though you yourself are dissatisfied with many things in it; it is all one, the climate is ripe and we must strike while the iron is hot.'[2] But the book was not completed immediately, for Marx felt the need to 'settle accounts with our erstwhile philosophical consciousness',[3] which he did in the *Holy Family* and *German Ideology*. By the summer of 1846 Leske lost patience and cancelled Marx's contract: Marx replied, in terms that were to become familiar, that the manuscript would be ready soon and would be much longer in consequence of his having to incorporate new material. Marx speaks there of two volumes of which 'the manuscripts – almost finished – of the first have been with me for a long time'.[4] This can only allude to the *Paris Manuscripts*. The second volume, on politics, which Marx describes as 'rather historical', would have dealt with the French Revolution among other things and incorporated the 1843 'Critique of Hegel's Political Philosophy'.[5] Later the same year, however, by joining the League of the Just, Marx started a period of active engagement in politics which, though it produced the *Poverty of Philosophy* and *Communist Manifesto* – the two books that Marx recommended as introductions to *Capital* – did not add to what he was to call his *Economics*.

After the failure of the 1848 Revolution, Marx once again took up his economic studies. He still believed in the imminence of a revolution, but considered that it would be dependent on the outbreak of an economic crisis. In the summer of 1850 Marx

---

[1] K. Marx, *Early Writings*, ed. Bottomore (London, 1963) p. 63.

[2] K. Marx, F. Engels, *Werke* (Berlin, 1957 ff.) (hereafter referred to as *MEW*) xxvii 16.

[3] K. Marx, F. Engels, *Selected Works* (Moscow, 1962) i 364.

[4] *MEW* xxvii 449.

[5] See the interesting table of contents that Marx drafted for this book, translated in *Writings of the Young Marx on Philosophy and Society*, ed. Easton and Guddat (New York, 1967) pp. 399 f.

obtained a ticket to the Reading Room of the British Museum,
and during the whole of 1851 got through an enormous amount
of reading : in January he was studying books on precious
metals, money and credit; in February, the economic writings of
Hume and Locke, and more books on money; in March, Ricardo,
Adam Smith and books on currencies; in April, Ricardo again and
books on money; in May, Carey, Malthus and principles of economics; in June, value, wealth and economics; in July, literature
on the factory system and agricultural incomes; in August, population, colonisation and the economics of the Roman world; in the
autumn, books on banking, agronomy and technology. In all,
Marx filled his notebooks with long passages from about eighty
authors and read many more. This study was directed towards the
completion of his work on economics. Already in January
1851 Engels was urging Marx to 'hurry up with the completion and publication of your *Economics*'.[1] By April Marx
wrote:

> I am so far advanced that in five weeks I will be through with
> the whole economic shit. And that done, I will work over my
> *Economics* at home and throw myself into another science in the
> Museum. I am beginning to be tired of it. Basically, this
> science had made no further progress since A. Smith and D.
> Ricardo, however much has been done in individual, often very
> subtle, researches.[2]

The book was eagerly awaited by Marx's friends. In May Lassalle
wrote:

> I have heard that your *Economics* will at last see the light of day
> . . . I am burning to contemplate on my desk the giant three-
> volume work of the Ricardo turned socialist and Hegel turned
> economist.[3]

Engels, however, who knew his friend well, declared that

> . . . as long as you still have unread a book that you think
> important, you do not get down to writing.[4]

---

[1] *MEW* xxvii 171.    [2] Ibid. 228.
[3] Lassalle to Marx, 12 May 1851.    [4] *MEW* xxvii 233 f.

In June, however, Marx was as sanguine as ever, writing to Weydemeyer:

> I am mostly in the Museum from nine in the morning until seven in the evening. The stuff I am working on has so many damned ramifications that with every effort I will not be able to finish for 6–8 weeks.[1]

Although Marx realised that 'one must at some point break off forcibly',[2] in July Proudhon's new book *The General Idea of Revolution in the Nineteenth Century* came into his hands and he immediately diverted his energies to criticising its contents. In spite of its anti-jacobinism, Proudhon's book appeared to Marx to deal with only the symptoms of capitalism and not its essence. However, by October friends had managed to interest the publisher Löwenthal in Marx's work. Marx's scheme for this work comprised three volumes: 'Critique of Economics', 'Socialism' and 'History of Economic Thought'. Löwenthal wished to begin with the last volume and see how it went. Engels urged Marx to accept this proposal, but to expand the 'History' into two volumes:

> After this would come the Socialists as the third volume and as fourth the Critique – what would be left of it – and the famous Positive, what you 'really' want. . . . For people of sufficient intelligence, the indications in the first volumes – the Anti-Proudhon and the Manifesto – will suffice to put them on the right track. The mass of buyers and readers will lose any interest in the 'History' if the great mystery is already revealed in the first volume. They will say, like Hegel in the *Phenomenology*: I have read the 'Preface' and that's where the general idea can be found.[3]

Engels advised Marx to make the book a long one by padding out the 'History' and finished: 'Show a little commercial sense this time.' In early December came the *coup d'état* of Bonaparte, which made Engels anticipate difficulties with Löwenthal and though Marx stayed in contact with him until well into the following year, nothing came of the negotiations. Even Marx's bitter enemy

---

[1] *MEW* xxvii 560.     [2] Ibid.     [3] Ibid. 373 f.

Kinkel was eager to get a 'positive foundation' from Marx's *Economics* and Lassalle proposed the founding of a company that would issue shares to finance the publication; but Marx doubted the success of the venture and anyway did not wish to make public his lack of resources. In January 1852 Marx wrote asking Weydemeyer to find him a publisher in America 'because of the failure in Germany'.[1] But Marx had already abandoned work on his *Economics*. He worked on his notebooks for a short period in the summer in 1852 and, as a last hope, submitted to the publisher Brockhaus the project of a book to be entitled *Modern Economic Literature in England from 1830 to 1852.* Brockhaus refused and Marx abandoned his *Economics* for several years.

In 1857, however, the long-predicted crisis did arrive, and moved Marx to take up again his economic studies. The first mention of this in his correspondence is a letter to Engels of December 1857 where he says: 'I am working madly through the nights on a synthesis of my economic studies, so that I at least have the main principles (*Grundrisse*) clear before the deluge.'[2] He was also composing an extremely detailed diary on the day-to-day events during the crisis.[3] The 'synthesis' that Marx speaks of here was already begun in August 1857 with the composition of a general introduction. This introduction, tentative in tone and incomplete, discusses the problem of method in the study of economics and attempts to justify the unhistorical order of the sections comprised in the work that was to follow.[4] A plan of these sections occurs at the end of the introduction, of which this is a slightly shortened version:

1. The general abstract characterisations that can more or less be applied to all types of society.
2. The categories that constitute the internal structure of bourgeois society and which serve as a basis for the fundamental classes. Capital, wage-labour, landed property. Their relationship to each other. Town and country. The three

---

[1] *MEW* xxviii 486.

[2] *MEW* xxix 225.

[3] Cf. Ibid. 232.

[4] It is reprinted as an appendix to *MEW* xi. Far too little attention is paid to this work in discussion of Marx written in English.

large social classes. The exchange between them. Circulation. Credit (private).

3. Synthesis of bourgeois society in the shape of the state. The state considered in itself. 'Unproductive' classes. Taxes. Public debt. Public credit. Population. Colonies. Emigration.

4. The international relations of production. International division of labour. International exchange. Exports and imports. Exchange rates.

5. The world market and crises.

This introduction was left unpublished. Marx wrote in 1859 in the preface to his *Critique of Political Economy*: 'I am omitting a general introduction which I had jotted down because on closer reflection any anticipation of results still to be proved appears to me to be disturbing, and the reader who on the whole desires to follow me must be resolved to ascend from the particular to the general.'[1] The plan, however, in a simpler form was reiterated in the same preface:

. . . capital, landed property, wage-labour; state, foreign trade, world market.[2]

The manuscripts which survive, written in the six months of October 1857 until March 1858, do not cover all these sections equally. They are obviously for the most part a draft of the first section of the *Economics*: the whole is divided into two parts, one on money and the second, much longer, on capital. The second part is divided into three sections on the production of capital, circulation, and conversion of surplus value into profit. However, these economic discussions are inextricably linked with digressions of a much wider nature on such subjects as the individual and society; the nature of labour; the influence of automation on society, problems of increasing leisure and the abolition of the division of labour; the nature of alienation in the higher stages of capitalist society; the revolutionary nature of capitalism and its inherent universality, and so on. It is these digressions that give the *Grundrisse* its primary importance and show that it is a rough

[1] Marx–Engels, *Selected Works* (Moscow, 1962) i 360.
[2] Ibid.

draft of far wider scope than what was later included in *Capital*. Sections devoted to such topics as foreign trade and the world market show that Marx was led to sketch out to some extent the fundamental traits of the other five books of his *Economics*. Marx says as much himself: 'In the manuscript (which would make a sizeable book if printed) everything is topsy-turvy and there is much that is intended for later parts.'[1]

The schema in six parts given in the general introduction and the preface is plainly not the same as that of *Capital*, book 1, published in 1867. Kautsky concluded that Marx must have changed the plan of his *Economics* and this has been the received opinion ever since. *Capital*, in its eventual four volumes, was held to be the form that Marx's *Economics* finally took and in it, to quote Engels, 'Marx said everything he wished in one way or another'. This question is obviously of the greatest importance. If true, then the *Grundrisse*, however interesting, would still only have a secondary importance, that of helping us to understand the genesis of *Capital* and thus to interpret its contents. If, on the other hand, Marx kept to the original plan and *Capital* is only the elaboration of the first of the six sections, then Marx's work is dramatically incomplete and it could be claimed that the *Grundrisse*, in so far as it is the *Grundrisse* of more than the first section, is the most fundamental work that Marx ever wrote.

The thesis that Marx changed the plan of his major work has been worked out in most detail by Henryk Grossmann.[2] He puts the date of the change in 1863, when Marx wrote to Engels that he had been obliged to 'destroy the whole edifice'.[3] But this sort of statement is far too frequent in Marx's correspondence to draw any important conclusions from it. Grossmann's main substantial point is that the plan of 1863 was methodologically different. There are two sources which show this view to be mistaken:[4]

[1] *MEW* xxix 330.

[2] Henryk Grossmann, 'Die Änderung des Aufbauplans des Marxschen Kapital', *Archiv für die Geschichte des Sozialismus und der Arbeiterbewegung* xiv (1929).

[3] *MEW* xxx 368.

[4] For what follows, see further the Basel dissertation of Otto Morf, *Das Verhältnis von Wissenschaftstheorie und Wirtschaftsgeschichte bei Karl Marx* (1951) pp. 75 ff. Also M. Rubel's introduction to K. Marx, *Œuvres*, ii (Paris, 1968) to which I am here, as elsewhere, much indebted.

1. *Marx's Correspondence*. This consists principally of letters to
Lassalle, who was acting as literary agent in the negotiations with
the prospective publisher Duncker. In February 1857 Marx listed
for the first time the six sections of his *Economics*: capital, landed
property, wage-labour, estate, foreign trade and the world market,
and added that the first section on capital would contain 'some
preliminary chapters'.[1] The arrangement with Duncker was that
the manuscript should be delivered and published in sections, and
the next month Marx informed Lassalle that the first delivery
would contain '(1) value, (2) money, (3) capital in general'. The
third section would be divided into 'the production process of
capital, the circulation of process of capital, and the unity of the
two, or capital and profit, interest'.[2] In other words, these sections
are precisely the subsequent three books of *Capital*. The change
is not one of methodology, but one of size; when it came to actually
writing the first of the six volumes, which Marx speaks of in his
letter to Lassalle as simply a 'brochure', it expanded to make the
three books of *Capital*.

2. The *Grundrisse*. In his March letter Marx promised to have
the first delivery ready by the 'end of May'.[3] It would be based on
materials which 'are only in my notebooks in the form of monographs, which often are very detailed; this would disappear at the
moment of composition'.[4] These materials are the *Grundrisse*,
whose 800 pages Marx had hoped to condense into the 'first
delivery'. The *Grundrisse* (which was not available to Grossmann
when he wrote his article) contains a further index which was to
be the basis of the first volume of Marx's *Economics*. This index
comprises: (1) value, (2) money (with subheadings in great detail),
(3) capital, divided once more into the process of production and
the process of circulation. This index proves beyond a doubt that
the plan of *Capital* was already in Marx's mind in 1857–8 as the
first of his six-volume treatise on *Economics*; and that the *Critique
of Political Economy* of 1859 contains what he refers to as 'some
preliminary chapters'.

By November 1858 the 'first delivery' was still not ready, but

[1] *MEW* xxix 554.      [2] Ibid.      [3] Ibid.      [4] Ibid.

Marx thought it would only be four weeks. Illness and journalism had taken up so much of his time, and particularly trouble with his liver had (according to him) affected his style. He wished to get everything right as '(1) my writing is the result of fifteen years of research, thus the best period of my life; (2) this work upholds for the first time in a scientific manner an important conception of the relationships in society'.[1] But, as could have been predicted, Marx found that he could not include all that he had to say on 'capital in general' in a single brochure: 'it is probable that the first part, "Capital in general", will already take up two brochures since in drafting it I find that just where the most abstract part of economics has to be discussed, too short a treatment would render it unintelligible to the public'.[2] At the same time, Marx insisted that both brochures should appear together: 'the inner connection demands it and the whole effect depends on it'.[3] However, lack of time obliged Marx to send the first brochure to Berlin or abandon the whole enterprise. He explained to Engels:

> In spite of the title 'Capital in general', these pages don't yet contain anything on capital, but only two chapters: (1) commodities, (2) money or simple circulation. You see therefore that the part elaborated in detail (in May when I was with you) will not yet be published.[4]

The heading of this first brochure was: 'Book 1. On capital. First section: Capital in general'. The plan in the *Grundrisse* shows that Marx intended, after finishing the section with the chapter on 'Capital in general', to add the further sections on more specific aspects of capital—circulation, credit, shares, etc., before proceeding to the other books on landed property, wage-labour and so on. This is spelt out even more clearly in a letter to Weydemeyer of February 1859.[5]

Even in October 1859 Marx still hoped to complete the second brochure, 'the true battle', by the end of the year. But journalism, domestic affairs and political quarrels – particularly the obscure

---

[1] *MEW* xxix 566.  [2] Ibid. 567.  [3] Ibid.
[4] Ibid. 383.  [5] Cf. Ibid. 572 f.

feud with Karl Vogt – ate into his time. In 1861 Marx did begin his 'third chapter' but found that in two years he had written about 3000 pages, a large part of which was edited by Kautsky as a sort of fourth volume to *Capital*, under the title of *Theories of Surplus Value*. In 1863 Marx began once more to work on the central thesis of his *Economics*, but it was seven years before this material emerged as *Capital: Book One* to be followed after Marx's death by books 2 and 3, the whole only constituting the first part of the total *Economics* that Marx in 1857 had intended to write.

Thus Marx's thought is best viewed as a continuing meditation on central themes broached in 1844, the high point of which meditation occurred in 1857–8. The continuity between the *Manuscripts* and *Grundrisse* is evident. Marx himself talked of the *Grundrisse* as 'the result of fifteen years of research, thus the best period of my life'.[1] This letter was written in November 1858, exactly fifteen years after Marx's arrival in Paris in November 1843. He also says in the preface of 1859: 'the total material lies before me in the form of monographs, which were written at widely separated periods, for self-clarification, not for publication, and whose coherent elaboration according to the plan indicated will be dependent on external circumstances'.[2] This can only refer to the *Paris Manuscripts* of 1844 and the London notebooks of 1850–2. Marx constantly used, and at the same time revised, material from an earlier date: he used his notebooks of 1843–5 while writing *Capital*.[3]

The beginning of the chapter on capital reproduces almost word for word the passages in the *Manuscripts* on human need, man as a species being, the individual as a social being, the idea of nature as, in a sense, man's body, the parallels between religious alienation and economic alienation, etc. The two works also have in common a Utopian and almost millennial strain. One point in particular emphasises this continuity: the *Grundrisse* is as 'Hegelian' as the *Paris Manuscripts*. This has sometimes been said to be a superficial Hegelianism, and Marx's letter to Engels of January 1858 has been quoted: 'in the *method* it has been of

---

[1] *MEW* xxix 566.

[2] Marx–Engels, *Selected Works* (Moscow, 1962) i 361.

[3] Cf. *MEW* xxix 330.

great use to me that by mere accident I have leafed through
Hegel's *Logic* – Freiligrath found some volumes that belonged
originally to Bakunin and sent me them as a present'.[1] The reading of Hegel may have been accidental but the influence of Hegel
went deeper: some of the most Hegelian parts of the *Grundrisse* –
and particularly the index of the book on capital – were written
*before* the receipt of Freiligrath's present. Marx himself, in a note
in the *Grundrisse* written in November 1858, said, 'later, before
going on to another problem, it is necessary to correct the idealist
manner of this analysis'. A parallel has justifiably been drawn
between the renewal of Marx's interest in Hegel and Lenin's
reading of Hegel that preceded the writing of his *Imperialism* and
*The State and Revolution*. The same point can be put with reference to the term 'alienation', which occurs much more in *Capital*
than some writers appear to think, and which is central to most
of the more important passages of the *Grundrisse*.

The most striking passage of the *Grundrisse* in this respect is
the draft plan for Marx's *Economics*, which is couched in language
(such as the distinction between essence and appearance) that
might have come straight out of Hegel's *Logic*.[2] Nor should the
obviously empirical nature of much of Marx's work cause a
problem. In a sense, Hegel himself was an extremely empirical
thinker and there is no contradiction between a close perusal of
the reports of the British factory inspectors and the Hegelian
categories used to interpret their significance. Since these sections
are typical of large parts of the *Grundrisse*, several of the accounts
of Marx's thought produced by scholars of the older generation –
Daniel Bell, Sidney Hook, Lewis Feuer[3] – must now be judged to
have been mistaken. It was the thesis of these writers that there
was a radical break between the young and the old Marx; and
the major proof of this was held to be the absence, in the later

[1] Ibid. 260. Freiligrath's letter offering Marx the volumes, dated 22 October
1857, has recently been published in *Freiligraths Briefwechsel mit Marx und Engels*
(Berlin, 1968) i 94.

[2] This is in contradistinction to the *Paris Manuscripts*, where it is Hegel's
*Phenomenology* that interests Marx most. See *Grundrisse*, 1953 ed., pp. 162 ff., and
particularly the schema on pp. 186f.

[3] Daniel Bell, 'The Debate on Alienation', *Revisionism* (1962); Sidney Hook,
*From Hegel to Marx*, 2nd ed. (1962); Lewis Feuer, 'What is Alienation? The Career
of a Concept', *New Politics* (1962).

writings, of the concept of alienation so central to the earlier writings. In addition those writers who have wished to minimise the influence of Hegel on Marx – this might apply to Rubel in some of his earlier work – will have to revise their ideas.

The richer historical content implies, too, that the *Grundrisse*, while continuing the themes central to the *Paris Manuscripts*, treats them in a much 'maturer' way than was possible before Marx had achieved a synthesis of his ideas on philosophy and economics. Thus those interpretations of Marx which take the *Paris Manuscripts* as his central work have seriously misplaced their emphasis. Eric Fromm and – to a lesser extent – Robert Tucker are examples of this tendency.[1] Equally, those critics of Marx who sometimes write as though Marx's summary of the 'guiding thread' of his studies in the preface to his *Critique of Political Economy* (1859) were a definite and exhaustive account of his views will have to do some wider reading.[2] For such a brief summary as is contained in the preface can only be adequately interpreted by reference to the immense amount of background thinking and writing from which it sprang.[3]

Marx never rejected any of his writings. It is, of course, true that he speaks of rereading the *Holy Family* with embarrassment. But this is true of all his writings: 'it is self evident', he wrote in 1846, 'that an author, if he pursues his research, cannot *literally* publish what he has written six months previously'.[4] Or in 1862: 'I find a work written four weeks before unsatisfactory and re-write it completely.'[5] In 1851 Marx was quite willing to see reprinted his essays from as long ago as the *Rheinische Zeitung* of 1842, and he states that even the *Communist Manifesto* was in need of amendment as time went on. Marx's intellectual develop-

---

[1] Eric Fromm, *Marx's Concept of Man* (1961); Robert Tucker, *Philosophy and Myth in Karl Marx* (1961).

[2] John Plamenatz, *German Marxism and Russian Communism* (1954); H. B. Acton, *The Illusion of the Epoch* (1955). But see further: H. B. Acton.

[3] See the article by A. Prinz in the *Journal of the History of Ideas* (1969), which argues that the preface was written solely with a view to getting Marx's book past the censors. This view seems to me untenable, but shows the sort of considerations that have to be borne in mind when commenting on such a text.

[4] *MEW* xxvii 449.

[5] *MEW* xxx 622.

ment is a process of 'self-clarification' (to use his own expression), which cannot either be split into periods or treated as a monolith. The central point of this process is neither the *Paris Manuscripts* nor *Capital*, but the *Grundrisse* of 1857–8, the work which, more than any other, contains a synthesis of the various strands of Marx's thought. When the young Kautsky asked Marx whether the time had not come to publish his complete works, Marx's wry answer was: 'They would first have to be completed.' In a sense, none of Marx's works is complete, but the completest of them is the *Grundrisse*.

# 1 General Introduction

From *Grundrisse*, pp. 5–31

*This is one of the first parts of the* Grundrisse *to be written, dated August 1857. Marx did not publish it in his* Critique of Political Economy *since 'any anticipation of results that are still to be proven seemed to me objectionable'. Marx begins with a critique of the eighteenth-century view of 'natural' man and the eternal laws supposed to govern economics by such writers as Mill. In the second section Marx considers the way in which production, distribution, exchange and consumption are intimately linked. The third section is particularly interesting for its discussion of method in political economy and the plan of the whole* Economics. *It ends with an unfinished digression on the appreciation of Greek art as an apparent difficulty for the materialist conception of history.*

*This text was first published by Karl Kautsky in 1903 and an English translation followed in 1904. This translation is far from satisfactory in many places and, though I have used it as a basis here, I have nevertheless amended it in many places.*

## 1. Production

THE subject of our discussion is first of all *material* production. Individuals producing in society, thus the socially determined production of individuals, naturally constitutes the starting point. The individual and isolated hunter or fisher who forms the starting point with Smith and Ricardo belongs to the insipid illusions of the eighteenth century. They are adventure stories which do not by any means represent, as students of the history of civilisation imagine, a reaction against over-refinement and a return to a misunderstood natural life. They are no more based on such a

naturalism than is Rousseau's *contrat social*, which makes naturally independent individuals come in contact and have mutual
intercourse by contract. They are the fiction and only the aesthetic
fiction of the small and great adventure stories. They are, rather,
the anticipation of 'civil society', which had been in course of
development since the sixteenth century and made gigantic
strides towards maturity in the eighteenth. In this society of free
competition the individual appears free from the bonds of nature,
etc., which in former epochs of history made him part of a definite,
limited human conglomeration. To the prophets of the eighteenth
century, on whose shoulders Smith and Ricardo are still standing,
this eighteenth-century individual, constituting the joint product
of the dissolution of the feudal form of society and of the new
forces of production which had developed since the sixteenth
century, appears as an ideal whose existence belongs to the past;
not as a result of history, but as its starting point. Since that
individual appeared to be in conformity with nature and corre-
sponded to their conception of human nature, he was regarded as
a product not of history but of nature. This illusion has been
characteristic of every new epoch in the past. Steuart, who, as an
aristocrat, stood more firmly on historical ground and was in many
respects opposed to the spirit of the eighteenth century, escaped
this simplicity of view.

The further back we go into history, the more the individual
and, therefore, the producing individual seems to depend on and
belong to a larger whole: at first it is, quite naturally, the family
and the clan, which is but an enlarged family; later on, it is the
community growing up in its different forms out of the clash and
the amalgamation of clans. It is only in the eighteenth century,
in 'civil society', that the different forms of social union confront
the individual as a mere means to his private ends, as an external
necessity. But the period in which this view of the isolated individual becomes prevalent is the very one in which the interrelations
of society (general from this point of view) have reached the
highest state of development. Man is in the most literal sense of
the word a *zoon politikon*, not only a social animal, but an animal
which can develop into an individual only in society. Production
by isolated individuals outside society – something which might
happen as an exception to a civilised man who by accident got

into the wilderness and already potentially possessed within himself the forces of society – is as great an absurdity as the idea of the development of language without individuals living together and talking to one another. We need not dwell on this any longer. It would not be necessary to touch upon this point at all, had not this nonsense – which however was justified and made sense in the eighteenth century – been transplanted, in all seriousness, into the field of political economy by Bastiat, Carey, Proudhon and others.   Proudhon and others naturally find it very pleasant, when they do not know the historical origin of a certain economic phenomenon, to give it a quasi-historico-philosophical explanation by going into mythology. Adam or Prometheus hit upon the scheme cut and dried, whereupon it was adopted, etc. Nothing is more tediously dry than the dreaming platitude.

Whenever we speak, therefore, of production, we always have in mind production at a certain stage of social development, or production by social individuals. Hence, it might seem that in order to speak of production at all, we must either trace the historical process of development through its various phases, or declare at the outset that we are dealing with a certain historical period, as, for example, with modern capitalist production, which, as a matter of fact, constitutes the proper subject of this work. But all stages of production have certain landmarks in common, common purposes. 'Production in general' is an abstraction, but it is a rational abstraction, in so far as it singles out and fixes the common features, thereby saving us repetition. Yet these general or common features discovered by comparison constitute something very complex, whose constituent elements have different destinations. Some of these elements belong to all epochs, others are common to a few. Some of them are common to the most modern as well as to the most ancient epochs. No production is conceivable without them; but while even the most completely developed languages have laws and conditions in common with the least developed ones, what is characteristic of their development are the points of departure from the general and common. The conditions which generally govern production must be differentiated in order that the essential points of difference should not be lost sight of in view of the general uniformity which is due to the fact that the subject, mankind, and the object, nature, remain the same. The failure to remember this one fact is the source of all the wisdom of modern economists who are trying to prove the eternal nature and harmony of existing social conditions. Thus they say, for example, that no production is possible without some instrument of production, let that instrument be only the hand; that none is possible without past accumulated labour, even if that labour should consist of mere skill which has been accumulated and concentrated in the hand of the savage by repeated exercise. Capital is, among other things, also an instrument of production, also past impersonal labour. Hence capital is a universal, eternal natural phenomenon; which is true if we disregard the specific properties which turn an 'instrument of production' and 'stored up labour' into capital. The entire history of the relationships of production appears to a man like Carey, for example, as a malicious perversion on the part of governments.

If there is no production in general there is also no general production. Production is always either some special branch of production, as, for example, agriculture, stock-raising, manufactures, etc., or an aggregate. But political economy is not technology. The connection between the general determinations of productions at a given stage of social development and the particular forms of production, is to be developed elsewhere (later on).

Finally, production is never only of a particular kind. It is always a certain social body or a social subject that is engaged on a larger or smaller aggregate of branches of production. The connection between the real process and its scientific presentation also falls outside of the scope of this treatise. Production in general. Special branches of production. Production as a whole.

It is the fashion with economists to open their works with a general introduction, which is entitled 'production' (see, for example, John Stuart Mill) and deals with the general 'requisites of production'. This general introductory part consists of (or is supposed to consist of):

1. The conditions without which production is impossible, i.e. the essential conditions of all production. As a matter of fact, however, it can be reduced, as we shall see, to a few very simple definitions, which flatten out into shallow tautologies.

2. Conditions which further production more or less, as, for example, Adam Smith's discussion of a progressive and stagnant state of society.

In order to give scientific value to what serves with him as a mere summary, it would be necessary to study the *degree of productivity* by periods in the development of individual nations; such a study falls outside the scope of the present subject, and in so far as it does belong here is to be brought out in connection with the discussion of competition, accumulation, etc. The commonly accepted view of the matter gives a general answer to the effect that an industrial nation is at the height of its production at the moment when it reaches its historical climax in all respects. As a matter of fact a nation is at its industrial height so long as its main object is not gain, but the process of gaining. In that respect the Yankees stand above the English. Or, that certain races, climates, natural conditions, such as distance from the sea, fertility of the soil, etc., are more favourable to production than others. That again comes down to the tautology that the facility of creating wealth depends on the extent to which its elements are present both subjectively and objectively.

But all that is not what the economists are really concerned with in this general part. Their object is rather to represent production in contradistinction to distribution – see Mill, for example – as subject to eternal laws independent of history, and then to substitute bourgeois relations, in an underhand way, as immutable natural laws of society *in abstracto*. This is the more or less conscious aim of the entire proceeding. When it comes to distribution, on the contrary, mankind is supposed to have indulged in all sorts of arbitrary action. Quite apart from the fact that they violently break the ties which bind production and distribution together, so much must be clear from the outset: that, no matter how greatly the systems of distribution may vary at different stages of society, it should be possible here, as in the case of production, to discover the common features and to confound and eliminate all historical differences in formulating *general human* laws. For example, the slave, the serf, the wage-labourer – all receive a quantity of food, which enables them to exist as slave, serf and wage-labourer. The conqueror, the official, the landlord, the monk or the Levite, who respectively live on tribute, taxes, rent, alms and the tithe – all receive a part of the social product which is determined by laws different from those which determine the part received by the slave, etc. The two main points which all economists place under this head are, first, property; second, the protection of the latter by the administration of justice, police, etc. The objections to these two points can be stated very briefly.

1. All production is appropriation of nature by the individual within and through a definite form of society. In that sense it is a tautology to say that property (appropriation) is a condition of production. But it becomes ridiculous, when from that one jumps at once to a definite form of property, e.g. private property (which implies, besides, as a prerequisite the existence of an opposite form, viz. absence of property). History points rather to common property (e.g. among the Hindus, Slavs, ancient Celts, etc.) as the primitive form, which still plays an important part at a much later period as communal property. The question as to whether wealth grows more rapidly under this or that form of property is not even raised here as yet. But that there can be no such thing as production, nor, consequently, society, where property does not exist in any form, is a tautology. Appropriation which does not appropriate is a *contradictio in subjecto*.

2. Protection of gain, etc. Reduced to their real meaning, these commonplaces express more than their preachers know, namely, that every form of production creates its own legal relations, forms of government, etc. The crudity and the shortcomings of the conception lie in the tendency to see only an accidental reflective connection in what constitutes an organic union. The bourgeois economists have a vague notion that production is better carried on under the modern police, than it was, for example, under club law. They forget that club law is also law, and that the right of the stronger continues to exist in other forms even under their 'government of law'.

When the social conditions corresponding to a certain stage of production are in a state of formation or disappearance, disturbances of production naturally arise, although differing in extent and effect.

To sum up: all the stages of production have certain destinations in common, which we generalise in thought; but the so-called general conditions of all production are nothing but abstract conceptions which do not go to make up any real stage in the history of production.

## 2. The General Relation of Production to Distribution, Exchange and Consumption

Before going into a further analysis of production, it is necessary to look at the various divisions which economists put side by side with it. The most shallow conception is as follows: By production, the members of society appropriate (produce and shape) the products of nature to human wants; distribution determines the proportion in which the individual participates in this production; exchange brings him the particular products into which he wishes to turn the quantity secured by him through distribution; finally through consumption the products become objects of use and enjoyment, of individual appropriation. Production yields goods adapted to our needs; distribution distributes them according to social laws; exchange distributes further what has already been distributed, according to individual wants; finally in consumption the product drops out of the social movement, becoming the direct object of the individual want which it serves and satisfies in use. Production thus appears as the starting point; consumption as the final end; and distribution and exchange as the middle; the latter has a double aspect, distribution being defined as a process carried on by society, exchange as one proceeding from the individual. The person is objectified in production; the material thing is subjectified in the person. In distribution, society assumes the part of go-between for production and consumption in the form of generally prevailing rules; in exchange this is accomplished by the accidental make-up of the individual.

Distribution determines what proportion (quantity) of the products the individual is to receive; exchange determines the products in which the individual desires to receive his share allotted to him by distribution.

Production, distribution, exchange and consumption thus form a perfect connection, production standing for the general, distribution and exchange for the special, and consumption for the individual, in which all are joined together. To be sure this is a connection, but it does not go very deep. Production is determined according to the economists by universal natural laws, while distribution depends on social chance: distribution can, therefore, have a more or less stimulating effect on production: exchange lies between the two as a formal social movement, and the final act of consumption, which is considered not only as a final purpose but also as a final aim, falls properly outside the scope of economics, except in so far as it reacts on the starting point and causes the entire process to begin all over again.

The opponents of the economists – whether economists themselves or not – who reproach them with tearing apart, like barbarians, what is an organic whole, either stand on common ground with them or are *below* them. Nothing is more common than the charge that the economists have been considering production as an end in itself, too much to the exclusion of everything else. The same has been said with regard to distribution. This accusation is itself based on the economic conception that distribution exists side by side with production as a self-contained, independent sphere. Or, it is said, the various factors are not grasped in their unity. As though it were the textbooks that impress this separation upon life and not life upon the textbooks; and as though the subject at issue were a dialectical balancing of conceptions and not an analysis of real conditions.

### a. Production Is at the Same Time Also Consumption

Twofold consumption, subjective and objective. The individual who develops his faculties in production is also expending them, consuming them in the act of production, just as procreation is a consumption of vital powers. In the second place, production is consumption of means of production which are used and used up and partly (as for example in burning) reduced to their natural elements. The same is true of the consumption of raw materials which do not remain in their natural form and state, being greatly absorbed in the process. The act of production is, therefore, in all its aspects an act of consumption as well. But this is admitted by economists. Production as directly identical with consumption, consumption as directly coincident with production,

they call productive consumption. This identity of production
and consumption finds its expression in Spinoza's proposition
*determinatio est negatio*. But this definition of productive consumption is resorted to just for the purpose of distinguishing
between consumption as identical with production and consumption proper, which is defined as its destructive counterpart. Let
us then consider consumption proper.

Consumption is directly also production, just as in nature the
consumption of the elements and of chemical substances constitutes production of plants. It is clear that in nutrition, for
example, which is but one form of consumption, man produces
his own body; but it is equally true of every kind of consumption
which goes to produce the human being in one way or another.
It is consumptive production. But, say the economists, this production which is identical with consumption is a second production resulting from the destruction of the product of the first. In
the first, the producer transforms himself into things; in the
second, things are transformed into human beings. Consequently,
this consumptive production – although constituting a direct
unity of production and consumption – differs essentially from
production proper. The direct unity in which production coincides with consumption and consumption with production does
not interfere with their direct duality.

Production is thus at the same time consumption, and consumption is at the same time production. Each is directly its own
counterpart. But at the same time an intermediary movement
goes on between the two. Production furthers consumption by
creating material for the latter which otherwise would lack its
object. But consumption in its turn furthers production, by providing for the products the individual for whom they are products.
The product receives its last finishing touches in consumption. A
railroad on which no one rides, which is consequently not used up,
not consumed, is only a potential railroad (or is a railway on
which no one travels) and not a real one. Without production,
no consumption; but, on the other hand, without consumption,
no production; since production would then be without a purpose.
Consumption produces production in two ways. In the first place,
in that the product first becomes a real product in consumption;
e.g. a garment becomes a real garment only through the act of

being worn; a dwelling which is not inhabited is really no dwelling; consequently, a product, as distinguished from a mere natural object, proves to be such, first *becomes* a product, in consumption. Consumption gives the product the finishing touch by annihilating it, since the result of production is a product, not as the material embodiment of activity but only as an object for the active subject.

In the second place, consumption produces production by creating the necessity for new production, i.e. by providing the ideal, inward, impelling cause which constitutes the prerequisite of production. Consumption furnishes the impulse for production as well as its object, which plays in production the part of its guiding aim. It is clear that while production furnishes the material object of consumption, consumption provides the ideal object of production, as its image, its want, its impulse and its purpose. It furnishes the objects of production in a form that is still subjective. No needs, no production. But consumption reproduces the need.

In its turn, production:

1. Furnishes consumption with its material, its object. Consumption without an object is no consumption, hence from this point of view production creates and produces consumption.

2. But it is not only the object that production provides for consumption. It gives consumption its definite outline, its character, its finish. Just as consumption gives the product its finishing touch as a product, production puts the finishing touch on consumption. For the object is not simply an object in general, but a definite object, which is consumed in a certain definite manner prescribed in its turn by production. Hunger is hunger; but the hunger that is satisfied with cooked meat eaten with fork and knife is a different kind of hunger from the one that devours raw meat with the aid of hands, nails and teeth. Not only the object of consumption, but also the manner of consumption is produced by production; that is to say, consumption is created by production not only objectively but also subjectively. Production thus creates the consumers.

3. Production not only supplies the want with material, but supplies the material with a want. When consumption emerges from its first stage of natural crudeness and directness – and its

continuation in that state would in itself be the result of a production still remaining in a state of natural crudeness – it is
itself, as a desire, mediated by its object. The want for it which
consumption experiences is created by its perception of the product. The object of art, as well as any other product, creates an
artistic public, appreciative of beauty. Production thus produces
not only an object for the subject, but also a subject for the object.

Production thus produces consumption: first, by furnishing
the latter with material; second, by determining the manner of
consumption; third, by creating in consumers a want for its
products as objects of consumption. It thus produces the object,
the manner and the desire for consumption. In the same manner,
consumption creates the *disposition* of the producer by setting
him up as an aim and by stimulating wants. The identity of
consumption and production thus appears to be a threefold one.

1. Direct identity: production is consumption; consumption is
production. Consumptive production. Productive consumption.
Economists call both productive consumption, but make one
distinction by calling the former reproduction, and the latter productive consumption. All inquiries into the former deal with
productive and unproductive labour; those into the latter treat
of productive and unproductive consumption.

2. Each appears as the means of the other and as being brought
about by the other, which is expressed as their mutual interdependence; a relation by virtue of which they appear as mutually
connected and indispensable, yet remaining external to each
other. Production creates the material as the external object of
consumption; consumption creates the want as the inward object,
the purpose of production. Without production, no consumption;
without consumption, no production; this maxim figures in political economy in many forms.

3. Production is not only directly consumption and consumption directly production; nor is production merely a means of
consumption and consumption the purpose of production. In
other words, not only does each furnish the other with its object:
production, the material object of consumption; consumption,
the imagined object of production. On the contrary, either one
is not merely directly the other, nor only a means of mediating the
other, but, while it completes itself, creates the other and itself

as the other. Consumption completes the act of production by giving the finishing touch to the product as such, by dissolving the latter, by breaking up its independent material form; by bringing to a state of readiness, through the necessity of repetition, the disposition to produce developed in the first act of production; that is to say, consumption is not only the concluding act through which the product becomes a product, but also the one through which the producer becomes a producer. On the other hand, production produces consumption, by determining the manner of consumption, and, further, by creating the incentive for consumption, the very ability to consume in the form of need. This latter identity, mentioned under point 3, is much discussed in political economy in connection with the treatment of the relations of demand and supply, of objects and needs, of natural needs and those created by society.

Hence, nothing is easier for a Hegelian than to treat production and consumption as identical. And this has been done not only by socialist writers of fiction, but even by economists, e.g. Say: the latter maintained that if we consider a nation as a whole, or mankind *in abstracto* – its production is at the same time its consumption. Storch pointed out Say's error by calling attention to the fact that a nation does not entirely consume its product, but also creates means of production, fixed capital, etc. To consider society as a single subject is moreover a false mode of speculative reasoning. For an individual, production and consumption appear as different aspects of one act. The important point to be emphasised here is that whether production and consumption are considered as activities of one individual or of separate individuals, they appear at any rate as aspects of one process in which production forms the actual starting point and is, therefore, the predominating factor. Consumption, as a natural necessity, as a want, constitutes an internal factor of productive activity, but the latter is the starting point of realisation and, therefore, its predominating factor, the act in which the entire process recapitulates itself. The individual produces a certain article and turns it again into himself by consuming it; but he returns as a productive and a self-reproducing individual. Consumption thus appears as a factor of production.

In society, however, the relation of the producer to his product, as soon as it is completed, is an outward one, and the return of the product to the individual depends on his relations to other individuals. He does not take immediate possession of it. Nor does the direct appropriation of the product constitute his purpose, when he produces in society. Between the producer and the product distribution steps in, determining by social laws his share in the world of products; that is to say, distribution steps in between production and consumption.

Does distribution form an independent sphere, standing side by side with and outside production?

### a. Production and Distribution

In reading the common treatises on economics one cannot help being struck by the fact that everything is treated there twice: e.g. under distribution there figure rent, wages, interest and profit; while under production we find land, labour and capital as agents of production. As regards capital, it is at once clear that it is counted twice: first, as an agent of production; second, as a source of income, as determining definite forms of distribution. Therefore interest and profit figure as such also in production, since they are forms in which capital increases and grows, and are consequently factors of its own production. Interest and profit, as forms of distribution, imply the existence of capital as an agent of production. They are forms of distribution which have for their prerequisite capital, as an agent of production. They are also forms of reproduction of capital.

Likewise, wages are wage-labour when considered under another head; the definite character which labour has in one case as an agent of production appears in the other as a form of distribution. If labour were not fixed as wage-labour, its manner of participation in distribution would not appear as wages, as is the case for example under slavery. Finally rent – to take at once the most developed form of distribution – by means of which landed property receives its share of the products, implies the existence of extensive landed property (properly speaking, agriculture on a large scale) as an agent of production, and not simply land, any more than wages simply imply labour. The relations and methods of distribution appear, therefore, merely as the reverse sides of the agents of production. An individual who participates in production as a wage-labourer receives his share of the products, i.e. of the results of production, in the form of wages. The subdivisions and organisation of distribution are determined by the subdivisions and organisation of production. Distribution is itself a product of production, not only in so far as the material goods are concerned, since only the results of production can be distributed; but also as regards its form, since the definite manner of participation in production determines the particular form of distribution, the form under which participation in distribution takes place. It is quite an illusion to place land under production, rent under distribution, etc.

Economists, like Ricardo, who are accused above all of having paid exclusive attention to production, define distribution, therefore, as the exclusive subject of political economy, because they instinctively regard the forms of distribution as the clearest forms in which the agents of production find expression in a given society.

To the single individual distribution naturally appears as a law established by society determining his position in the sphere of production, within which he produces, and thus antedating production. At the outset the individual has no capital, no landed property. From his birth he is assigned to wage-labour by the social process of distribution. But this very condition of being assigned to wage-labour is the result of the existence of capital and landed property as independent agents of production.

From the point of view of society as a whole, distribution seems to antedate and to determine production in another way as well, as a pre-economic fact, so to speak. A conquering people divides the land among the conquerors, establishing thereby a certain division and form of landed property and determining the character of production; or it turns the conquered people into slaves and thus makes slave labour the basis of production. Or a nation, by revolution, breaks up large estates into small parcels of land and by this new distribution imparts to production a new character. Or legislation perpetuates land ownership in large families or distributes labour as a hereditary privilege and thus fixes it in castes. In all of these cases, and they are all historic, it is not distribution that seems to be organised and determined by production but, on the contrary, production by distribution.

In the most shallow conception of distribution, the latter appears as a distribution of products and, to that extent, as further removed from and quasi-independent of production. But before distribution means distribution of products, it is, first, a distribution of the means of production, and secondly, which is another determination of the same relationship, it is a distribution of the members of society among the various kinds of production (the subjection of individuals to certain relationships of production). The distribution of products is manifestly only a result of this distribution, which is bound up with the process of production and determines the organisation of the latter. To treat of production apart from the distribution which is comprised in it is plainly an idle abstraction. Conversely, we know the character of the distribution of products the moment we are given the nature of that other distribution which forms originally a factor of production. Ricardo, who was concerned with the analysis of production as it is organised in modern society and who was the economist of production *par excellence*, for that very reason declares *not* production but distribution to be the proper subject of modern economics. We have here another evidence of the insipidity of the economists who treat production as an eternal truth, and banish history to the domain of distribution.

What relation to production this distribution, which has a determining influence on production itself, assumes, is plainly a question which falls within the province of production. Should it be maintained that, at least to the extent that production depends on a certain distribution of the instruments of production, distribution in that sense precedes production and constitutes its prerequisite, it may be replied that production has in fact its prerequisite conditions, which form factors of it. These may appear at first to have a natural, spontaneous origin. By the very process of production they are changed from natural to historical, and if they appear during one period as a natural prerequisite of production, they formed at other periods its historical result. Within the sphere of production itself they undergo a constant change. For example the application of machinery produces a change in the distribution of the instruments of production as well as in that of products, and modern land ownership on a large scale is as much the result of modern trade and modern industry as that of the application of the latter to agriculture.

All these questions resolve themselves in the last instance to this: How do general historical conditions affect production and what part does it play at all in the course of history? It is evident that this question can be taken up only in connection with the discussion and analysis of production.

Yet in the trivial form in which these questions are raised above, they can be answered just as briefly. In the case of all conquests three ways lie open. The conquering people may impose its own methods of production upon the conquered (e.g. the English in Ireland in the nineteenth century, partly also in India); or it may allow everything to remain as it was, contenting itself with tribute (e.g. The Turks and the Romans); or the two systems by mutually modifying each other may result in something new, a synthesis (which partly resulted from the Germanic conquests). In all these conquests the method of production, be it that of the conquerors, the conquered, or the one resulting from a combination of both, determines the nature of the new distribution which comes into play. Although the latter appears now as the prerequisite condition of the new period of production, it is in itself but a product of production, not only of production belonging to history in general, but of production relating to a definite historical period. The Mongols with their devastations in Russia, for example, acted in accordance with their system of production, for which sufficient pastures on large uninhabited stretches of country are the main prerequisite. The Germanic barbarians, for whom agriculture carried on with the aid of serfs was the traditional system of production and who were accustomed to a lonely life in the country, could introduce the same conditions in the Roman provinces so much the more easily since the concentration of landed property which had taken place there did away completely with the older systems of agriculture. There is a prevalent tradition that in certain periods robbery constituted the only source of living. But in order to be able to plunder, there must be something to plunder, i.e. there must be production. And even the method of plunder is determined by the method of production. A stock-jobbing nation, for example, cannot be robbed in the same manner as a nation of shepherds.

In the case of the slave the instrument of production is robbed directly. But then the production of the country in whose interest he is robbed must be so organised as to admit of slave labour, or (as in South America, etc.) a system of production must be introduced adapted to slavery.

Laws may perpetuate an instrument of production, e.g. land, in certain families. These laws only assume an economic importance if extensive landed property is in harmony with the system of production prevailing in society, as is the case for example in England. In France agriculture had been carried on on a small scale in spite of the large estates, and the latter were, therefore, broken up by the Revolution. But how about the legislative attempt to perpetuate the minute subdivision of the land? In spite of these laws land ownership is concentrating again. The effect of legislation on the maintenance of a system of distribution and its resultant influence on production must be made particularly clear.

### c. *Exchange and Circulation*

Circulation is but a certain aspect of exchange, or it may be defined as exchange considered as a whole. Since *exchange* is an intermediary factor between production and its dependant, distribution, on the one hand, and consumption on the other, and since the latter appears only as a constituent of production, exchange is manifestly also a constituent part of production.

In the first place, it is clear that the exchange of activities and abilities which takes place in the sphere of production falls directly within the latter and constitutes one of its essential elements. In the second place, the same is true of the exchange of products, in so far as it is a means of completing a certain product designed for immediate consumption. To that extent exchange constitutes an act included in production. Thirdly, the so-called exchange between dealers and dealers is by virtue of its organisation determined by production, and is itself a species of productive activity. Exchange appears to be independent of and indifferent to production only in the last stage, when products are exchanged directly for consumption. But in the first place, there is no exchange without a division of labour, whether natural or as a result of historical development; secondly, private exchange implies the existence of private production; thirdly, the intensity of exchange, as well as its extent and character, are determined by the degree of development and organisation of production, as for example exchange between city and country, exchange in the country, in the city, etc. Exchange thus appears in all its aspects to be directly included in or determined by production.

The result we arrive at is not that production, distribution, exchange and consumption are identical, but that they are all members of one entity, different aspects of one unit. Production predominates not only over production itself in the opposite sense of that term, but over the other elements as well. With production the process constantly starts over again. That exchange and consumption cannot be the predominating elements is self-evident. The same is true of distribution in the narrow sense of distribution of products; as for distribution in the sense of distribution of the agents of production, it is itself but a factor of production. A definite form of production thus determines the forms of consumption, distribution, exchange and *also the mutual relations between these various elements*. Of course, production *in its one-sided form* is in its turn influenced by other elements, e.g. with the expansion of the market, i.e. of the sphere of exchange, production grows in volume and is subdivided to a greater extent.

With a change in distribution, production undergoes a change; as for example in the case of concentration of capital, of a change in the distribution of population in city and country, etc. Finally the demands of consumption also influence production. A mutual interaction takes place between the various elements. Such is the case with every organic body.

## 3. The Method of Political Economy

When we consider a given country from a politico-economic standpoint, we begin with its population, its subdivision into classes, location in city, country or by the sea, occupation in different branches of production; then we study its exports and imports, annual production and consumption, prices of commodities, etc. It seems to be the correct procedure to commence with the real and the concrete, the actual prerequisites; in the case of political economy, to commence with population, which is the basis and the author of the entire productive activity of society. Yet on closer consideration it proves to be wrong. Population is an abstraction, if we leave out for example the classes of which it consists. These classes, again, are but an empty word unless we know what are the elements on which they are based, such as wage-labour, capital, etc. These imply, in their turn, exchange, division of labour, prices, etc. Capital, for example, does not mean anything without wage-labour, value, money, price, etc. If we start out, therefore, with population, we do so with a chaotic conception of the whole, and by closer analysis we will gradually arrive at simpler ideas; thus we shall proceed from the imaginary concrete to less and less complex abstractions, until we arrive at the simplest determinations. This once attained, we might start on our return journey until we finally came back to population, but this time not as a chaotic notion of an integral whole, but as a rich aggregate of many determinations and relations. The former method is the one which political economy had adopted in the past as its inception. The economists of the seventeenth century, for example, always started out with the living aggregate: population, nation, state, several states, etc., but in the end they invariably arrived by means of analysis at certain leading abstract general principles such as division of labour, money, value, etc. As soon as these separate elements had been more or less established by abstract reasoning, there arose the systems of political economy which start from simple conceptions such as labour, division of labour, demand, exchange value, and conclude with state, international exchange and world market. The latter is manifestly the scientifically correct method. The concrete is concrete because it is a combination of many determinations, i.e. a unity of diverse elements. In our thought it therefore appears as a process of synthesis, as a result, and not as a starting point, although it is the real starting point and, therefore, also the starting point of observation and conception. By the former method the complete conception passes into an abstract definition; by the latter the abstract definitions lead to the reproduc-

tion of the concrete subject in the course of reasoning. Hegel fell
into the error, therefore, of considering the real as the result of
self-co-ordinating, self-absorbed and spontaneously operating
thought, while the method of advancing from the abstract to the
concrete is but the way of thinking by which the concrete is
grasped and is reproduced in our mind as concrete. It is by no
means, however, the process which itself generates the concrete.
The simplest economic category, say, exchange value, implies the
existence of population, population that is engaged in production
under certain conditions; it also implies the existence of certain
types of family, clan or state, etc. It can have no other existence
except as an abstract one-sided relation of an already given
concrete and living aggregate.

As a category, however, exchange value leads an antediluvian
existence. Thus the consciousness for which comprehending
thought is what is most real in man, for which the world is only
real when comprehended (and philosophical consciousness is of
this nature), mistakes the movement of categories for the real act
of production (which unfortunately receives only its impetus from
outside), whose result is the world; that is true – here we have,
however, again a tautology – in so far as the concrete aggregate,
as a thought aggregate, the concrete subject of our thought, is in
fact a product of thought, of comprehension; not, however, in the
sense of a product of a self-emanating conception which works
outside of and stands above observation and imagination, but of
a conceptual working-over of observation and imagination. The
whole, as it appears in our heads as a thought-aggregate, is the
product of a thinking mind which grasps the world in the only
way open to it, a way which differs from the one employed by the
artistic, religious or practical mind. The concrete subject continues to lead an independent existence after it has been grasped,
as it did before, outside the head, so long as the head contem-
plates it only speculatively, theoretically. So that in the employ-
ment of the theoretical method in political economy, the subject,
society, must constantly be kept in mind as the premise from
which we start.

But have these simple categories no independent historical or
natural existence antedating the more concrete ones? That
depends. For instance in his *Philosophy of Right* Hegel rightly

starts out with possession, as the simplest legal relation of individuals. But there is no such thing as possession before the family or the relations of lord and serf, which relations are a great deal more concrete, have come into existence. On the other hand, one would be right in saying that there are families and clans which only *possess*, but do not *own* things. The simpler category thus appears as a relation of simple family and clan communities with respect to property. In society the category appears as a simple relation of a developed organisation, but the concrete substratam from which the relation of possession springs is always implied. One can imagine an isolated savage in possession of things. But in that case possession is no legal relation. It is not true that the family came as the result of the historical evolution of possession. On the contrary, the latter always implies the existence of this 'more concrete category of law'. Yet this much may be said, that the simple categories are the expression of relations in which the less developed concrete entity may have been realised without entering into the manifold relations and bearings which are mentally expressed in the concrete category; but when the concrete entity attains fuller development it will retain the same category as a subordinate relation.

Money may exist and actually had existed in history before capital or banks or wage-labour came into existence. With that in mind, it may be said that the more simple category can serve as an expression of the predominant relations of an undeveloped whole or of the subordinate relations of a more developed whole, relations which had historically existed before the whole developed in the direction expressed in the more concrete category. To this extent, the course of abstract reasoning, which ascends from the most simple to the complex, corresponds to the actual process of history.

On the other hand, it may be said that there are highly developed but historically less mature forms of society in which the highest economic forms are to be found, such as co-operation, advanced division of labour, etc., and yet there is ńo money in existence, e.g. Peru. In Slav communities also, money, as well as exchange to which it owes its existence, does not appear at all or very little within the separate communities, but it appears on their boundaries in their intercommunal traffic; in general, it is erroneous to consider exchange as a constituent element originating within the community. It appears at first more in the mutual relations between different communities than in those between the members of the same community. Furthermore, although money begins to play its part everywhere at an early stage, it plays in antiquity the part of a predominant element only in unidirectionally developed nations, viz. trading nations, and even in the most cultured antiquity, in Greece and Rome, it attains its full development, which constitutes the prerequisite of modern bourgeois society, only in the period of their decay. Thus this quite simple category attained its culmination in the past only at the most advanced stages of society. Even then it did not pervade all economic relations; in Rome for example at the time of its highest development, taxes and payments in kind remained the basis. As a matter of fact, the money system was fully developed there only so far as the army was concerned; it never came to dominate the entire system of labour. Thus, although the simple category may have existed historically before the more concrete one, it can attain its complete internal and external development only in complex forms of society, while the more concrete category has reached its full development in a less advanced form of society.

Labour is quite a simple category. The idea of labour in that sense, as labour in general, is also very old. Yet 'labour' thus simply defined by political economy is as much a modern category as the conditions which have given rise to this simple abstraction. The monetary system, for example, defines wealth quite objectively, as a thing external to itself in money. Compared with this point of view, it was a great step forward when the industrial or commercial system came to see the source of wealth not in the object but in the activity of persons, viz. in commercial and industrial labour. But even the latter was thus considered only in the limited sense of a money-producing activity. The physiocratic system marks still further progress in that it considers a certain form of labour, viz. agriculture, as the source of wealth, and wealth itself not in the disguise of money, but as a product in general, as the general result of labour. But corresponding to the limitations of the activity, this product is still only a natural product. Agriculture is productive, land is the source of production *par excellence.* It was a tremendous advance on the part of Adam Smith to throw aside all the limitations which mark wealth-producing activity and to define it as labour in general, neither industrial nor commercial nor agricultural, or one as much as the other. Along with the universal character of wealth-creating activity we now have the universal character of the object defined as wealth, viz. product in general, or labour in general, but as past, objectified labour. How difficult and how great was the transition is evident from the way Adam Smith himself falls back from time to time into the physiocratic system. Now it might seem as though this amounted simply to finding an abstract expression for the simplest relation into which men have been mutually entering as producers from times of yore, no matter under what form of society. In one sense this is true. In another it is not.

The indifference as to the particular kind of labour implies the existence of a highly developed aggregate of different species of concrete labour, none of which is any longer the predominant one. So the most general abstractions commonly arise only where there is the highest concrete development, where one feature appears to be jointly possessed by many and to be common to all. Then it cannot be thought of any longer in one particular form. On the other hand, this abstraction of labour is only the result of a concrete aggregate of different kinds of labour. The indifference to the particular kind of labour corresponds to a form of society in which individuals pass with ease from one kind of work to another, which makes it immaterial to them what particular kind of work may fall to their share. Labour has become here, not only categorially but really, a means of creating wealth in general and has no longer coalesced with the individual in one particular manner. This state of affairs has found its highest development in the most modern of bourgeois societies, the United States. It is only here that the abstraction of the category 'labour', 'labour in general', labour *sans phrase*, the starting point of modern political economy, becomes realised in practice. Thus the simplest abstraction which modern political economy sets up as its starting point, and which expresses a relation dating back to antiquity and prevalent under all forms of society, appears truly realised in this abstraction only as a category of the most modern society. It might be said that what appears in the United States as a historical product – viz. the indifference as to the particular kind of labour – appears among the Russians, for example, as a spontaneously natural disposition. But it makes all the difference in the world whether barbarians have a natural predisposition which makes them applicable alike to everything, or whether civilised people apply themselves to everything. And, besides, this indifference of the Russians as to the kind of work they do corresponds to their traditional practice of remaining in the rut of a quite definite occupation until they are thrown out of it by external influences.

This example of labour strikingly shows how even the most abstract categories, in spite of their applicability to all epochs – just because of their abstract character – are by the very definiteness of the abstraction a product of historical conditions as well, and are fully applicable only to and under those conditions.

Bourgeois society is the most highly developed and most highly differentiated historical organisation of production. The categories which serve as the expression of its conditions and the comprehension of its own organisation enable it at the same time to gain an insight into the organisation and the relationships of production which have prevailed under all the past forms of society, on the ruins and constituent elements of which it has arisen, and of which it still drags along some unsurmounted remains, while what had formerly been mere intimation has now developed to complete significance. The anatomy of the human being is the key to the anatomy of the ape. But the intimations of a higher animal in lower ones can be understood only if the animal of the higher order is already known. The bourgeois economy furnishes a key to ancient economy, etc. This is, however, by no means true of the method of those economists who blot out all historical differences and see the bourgeois form in all forms of society. One can understand the nature of tribute, tithes, etc., after one has learned the nature of rent. But they must not be considered identical.

Since, furthermore, bourgeois society is only a form resulting from the development of antagonistic elements, some relations belonging to earlier forms of society are frequently to be found in it, though in a crippled state or as a travesty of their former self, as for example communal property. While it may be said, therefore, that the categories of bourgeois economy contain what is true of all other forms of society, the statement is to be taken *cum grano salis*. They may contain these in a developed or crippled or caricatured form, but always essentially different. The so-called historical development amounts in the last analysis to this, that the last form considers its predecessors as stages leading up to itself and always perceives them from a single point of view, since it is very seldom and only under certain conditions that it is capable of self-criticism; of course, we do not speak here of such historical periods as appear to their own contemporaries to be periods of decay. The Christian religion became capable of assisting us to an objective view of past mythologies as soon as it was ready for self-criticism to a certain extent, *dynamei*, so to speak. In the same way bourgeois political economy first came to understand the feudal, the ancient and the oriental societies as soon as the self-criticism of bourgeois society had commenced. In as far as bourgeois political economy has not gone into the mythology of identifying the bourgeois system purely with the past, its criticism of the feudal system against which it still had to wage war resembled Christian criticism of the heathen religions or Protestant criticism of Catholicism.

In the study of economic categories, as in the case of every historical and social science, it must be borne in mind that, as in reality so in our mind, the subject, in this case modern bourgeois society, is given, and that the categories are therefore only forms of being, manifestations of existence, and frequently only one-sided aspects of this subject, this definite society; and that, expressly for that reason, the origin of political economy *as a science* does not by any means date from the time to which it is referred to *as such*. This is to be firmly kept in mind because it has an immediate and important bearing on the matter of the subdivisions of the science.

For instance, nothing seems more natural than to start with rent, with landed property, since it is bound up with land, the source of all production and all existence, and with the first form of production in all more or less settled communities, viz. agriculture. But nothing would be more erroneous. Under all forms of society there is a certain industry which predominates over all the rest and whose condition therefore determines the rank and influence of all the rest.

It is the universal light with which all the other colours are tinged and by whose peculiarity they are modified. It is a special ether which determines the specific gravity of everything that appears in it.

Let us take for example pastoral nations (mere hunting and fishing tribes are not as yet at the point from which real development commences). They engage in a certain form of agriculture, sporadically. The nature of land-ownership is determined thereby. It is held in common and retains this form more or less according to the extent to which these nations hold on to traditions; such, for example, is land ownership among the Slavs. Among nations whose agriculture is carried on by a settled population – the settled state constituting a great advance – where agriculture is the predominant industry, such as in ancient and feudal societies, even the manufacturing industry and its organisations, as well as the forms of property which pertain to it, have more or less the characteristic features of the prevailing system of land ownership; society is then either entirely dependent upon agriculture, as in the case of ancient Rome, or, as in the Middle Ages, it imitates in its civic relations the forms of organisation prevailing in the country. Even capital, with the exception of pure money capital, has, in the form of the traditional working tool, the characteristics of land ownership in the Middle Ages.

The reverse is true of bourgeois society. Agriculture comes to be more and more merely a branch of industry and is completely dominated by capital. The same is true of rent. In all the forms of society in which land ownership is the prevalent form, the influence of the natural element is the predominant one. In those where capital predominates, the prevailing element is the one historically created by society. Rent cannot be understood without capital, whereas capital can be understood without rent. Capital is the all-dominating economic power of bourgeois society. It must form the starting point as well as the end and be developed before land ownership. After each has been considered separately, their mutual relation must be analysed.

It would thus be impractical and wrong to arrange the economic categories in the order in which they were the determining factors in the course of history. Their order of sequence is rather determined by the relation which they bear to one another in modern bourgeois society, and which is the exact opposite of what seems to be their natural order or the order of their historical development. What we are interested in is not the place which economic relations occupy in the historical succession of different forms of society. Still less are we interested in the order of their succession 'in the idea' (*Proudhon*), which is but a hazy conception of the course of history. We are interested in their organic connection within modern bourgeois society.

The sharp line of demarcation (abstract precision) which so clearly distinguished the trading nations of antiquity, such as the Phoenicians and the Carthaginians, was due to that very predominance of agriculture. Capital as trading or money capital appears in that abstraction where capital does not constitute as yet the predominating element of society. The Lombards and the Jews occupied the same position among the agricultural societies of the Middle Ages.

As a further illustration of the fact that the same category plays different parts at different stages of society, we may mention the following: one of the latest forms of bourgeois society, viz. joint stock companies, appear also at its beginning in the form of the great chartered monopolistic trading companies.

The concept of national wealth which is imperceptibly formed in the minds of the economists of the seventeenth century, and which in part continues to be entertained by those of the eighteenth century, is that wealth is produced solely for the state, but that the power of the latter is proportional to that wealth. It was as yet an unconsciously hypocritical way in which wealth announced itself and its own production as the aim of modern states, considering the latter merely as a means to the production of wealth.

The order of treatment must manifestly be as follows: first, the general abstract definitions which are more or less applicable to all forms of society, but in the sense indicated above. Second, the categories which go to make up the inner organisation of bourgeois society and constitute the foundations of the principal classes: capital, wage-labour, landed property; their mutual relations; city and country; the three great social classes, the exchange between them; circulation, credit (private). Third, the organisation of bourgeois society in the form of the state, considered in relation to itself; the 'unproductive' classes; taxes; public debts; public credit; population; colonies; emigration. Fourth, the international organisation of production; international division of labour; international exchange; import and export; rate of exchange. Fifth, the world market and crises.

## 4. Production, Means of Production and Conditions of Production: The Relations of Production and Distribution; The Connection Between Form of State and Consciousness on the One Hand and Relations of Production and Distribution on the Other: Legal Relations: Family Relations

Notes on the points to be mentioned here and not to be omitted:

1. *War* attains complete development before peace; how certain economic phenomena, such as wage-labour, machinery, etc., are developed at an earlier date through war and in armies than within bourgeois society. The connection between productive force and commercial relationships is made especially plain in the case of the army.

2. The relation between the previous idealistic methods of writing history and the realistic method; namely, the so-called history of civilisation, which is all a history of religion and states. In this connection something may be said of the different methods hitherto employed in writing history. The so-called objective method. The subjective (the moral and others). The philosophical.

3. *Secondary and tertiary.* Conditions of production which have been taken over or transplanted; in general, those that are not original. Here the effect of international relations must be introduced.

4. Objections to the materialistic character of this view. Its relation to naturalistic materialism.

5. The dialectic of the conceptions of productive force (means of production) and relation of production, a dialectic whose

limits are to be determined and which does not do away with the concrete difference.

6. The unequal relation between the development of material production and art, for instance. In general, the conception of progress is not to be taken in the sense of the usual abstraction. In the case of art, etc., it is not so important and difficult to understand this disproportion as in that of practical social relations, e.g. the relation between education in the United States and Europe. The really difficult point, however, that is to be discussed here is that of the unequal development of relations of production as legal relations. As, for example, the connection between Roman civil law (this is less true of criminal and public law) and modern production.

7. This conception of development appears to imply necessity. On the other hand, justification of accident. How. (Freedom and other points.) (The effect of means of communication.) World history has not always existed; history as world history is a result.

8. The starting point is to be found in certain facts of nature embodied subjectively and objectively in clans, races, etc.

It is well known that certain periods of the highest development of art stand in no direct connection to the general development of society, or to the material basis and skeleton structure of its organisation. Witness the example of the Greeks as compared with the modern nations, or even Shakespeare. As regards certain forms of art, e.g. the epos, it is admitted that they can never be produced in the universal epoch-making form as soon as art as such has come into existence; in other words, that in the domain of art certain important forms of it are possible only at a low stage of its development. If that be true of the mutual relations of different forms of art within the domain of art itself, it is far less surprising that the same is true of the relation of art as a whole to the general development of society. The difficulty lies only in the general formulation of these contradictions. No sooner are they specified than they are explained.

Let us take for instance the relation of Greek art, and that of Shakespeare's time, to our own. It is a well-known fact that Greek mythology was not only the arsenal of Greek art, but also the very ground from which it had sprung. Is the view of nature and of social relations which shaped Greek imagination and Greek art

possible in the age of automatic machinery and railways and locomotives and electric telegraphs? Where does Vulcan come in as
against Roberts & Co.? Jupiter, as against the lightning con-
ductor? and Hermes, as against the *Crédit Mobilier*? All mythology masters and dominates and shapes the forces of nature in and
through the imagination; hence it disappears as soon as man
gains mastery over the forces of nature. What becomes of the
Goddess Fama side by side with Printing House Square? Greek
art presupposes the existence of Greek mythology, i.e. that nature
and even the form of society are wrought up in popular fancy in an
unconsciously artistic fashion. That is its material. Not, however,
any mythology taken at random, nor any accidental unconsciously
artistic elaboration of nature (including under the latter all
objects, hence also society). Egyptian mythology could never be
the soil or womb which would give birth to Greek art. But in any
event there had to be a mythology. In no event could Greek art
originate in a society which excludes any mythological explanation
of nature, any mythological attitude towards it, or which requires
of the artist an imagination free from mythology.

Looking at it from another side: is Achilles possible side by
side with powder and lead? Or is the *Iliad* at all compatible with
the printing press and even printing machines? Do not singing
and reciting and the muses necessarily go out of existence with
the appearance of the printer's bar, and do not, therefore, the
prerequisites of epic poetry disappear?

But the difficulty is not in grasping the idea that Greek art and
epos are bound up with certain forms of social development. It
lies rather in understanding why they still constitute for us a
source of aesthetic enjoyment and in certain respects prevail as
the standard and model beyond attainment.

A man cannot become a child again unless he becomes childish.
But does he not enjoy the artless ways of the child, and must he
not strive to reproduce its truth on a higher plane? Is not the
character of every epoch revived, perfectly true to nature, in the
child's nature? Why should the childhood of human society,
where it had obtained its most beautiful development, not exert
an eternal charm as an age that will never return? There are
ill-bred children and precocious children. Many of the ancient
nations belong to the latter class. The Greeks were normal

children. The charm their art has for us does not conflict with the primitive character of the social order from which it had sprung. It is rather the product of the latter, and is due rather to the fact that the immature social conditions under which the art arose and under which alone it could appear can never return.

# 2 Critique of Bastiat and Carey

From *Grundrisse*, pp. 843–53

*This is the first of the manuscripts of the* Grundrisse *written by Marx, dating from July 1857. The two books concerned are: Frédéric Bastiat,* Harmonies économiques, *2nd ed. (Paris, 1851), and Henry Carey,* Principles of Political Economy *(Philadelphia, 1837). Marx portrays Bastiat and Carey as incarnating respectively the vices (and virtues) of the disciples of Proudhon and the mid-nineteenth century Yankee.*

J ust as the history of modern political economy began at the end of the seventeenth century with Petty and Boisguillebert, so it ends with Ricardo and Sismondi, two opposite poles, of whom one spoke English and the other French. Later, political economic literature lost its way either in eclectic, syncretic compendiums, like the work of J. S. Mill for example, or in the more detailed elaboration of individual branches, such as Tooke's *History of Prices*, and, in general, recent English publications on circulation – the only branch in which really new discoveries have been made. As for publications on colonisation, landed property (in its various forms), population, etc., they can really only be distinguished from older works by their greater volume of material; or else they re-discuss old economic problems for a wider public in order to provide a practical solution to problems of the day, such as writings on free trade and protection; or, finally, they lend tendentious exaggeration to the ideas of classical economists, as Chalmers does in relation to Malthus, and Gulich to Sismondi, and to a certain extent MacCulloch and Senior in their earlier writings in relation to Ricardo. This is nothing but a literature composed by epigoni, a literature of repetition, of formal elaboration, of a wider and more captious appropriation of the material, of popularisation, summarising and working out of details. This literature shows no crucial, decisive phases of development, and embodies a mere inventory on one side, and excessive detail on the other.

It appears that only the work of the American Carey and the Frenchman Bastiat form an exception to this, the latter admitting that he is dependent on the former. Both of them have understood that the opponents of political economy – socialism and communism – find their theoretical basis in the work of classical economies, especially in Ricardo, who must be considered as its most perfect and final expression. Both of them find it therefore necessary to attack the theoretical expression that bourgeois society has attained historically in modern economics by presenting it as a misunderstanding, and to demonstrate the harmony of the conditions of production which the classical economists had naïvely described as antagonistic. Despite the very different and even contradictory national background from which they write, the aspirations to which they are led are none the less the same. Carey is the only original North American economist. He belongs to a country in which bourgeois society has not developed from a background of feudalism, but began of its own accord; a country where this society was not the surviving result of centuries of development, but the starting point of a new movement; where the state, unlike all other national structures, was from the start subordinated to bourgeois society and to bourgeois production, and could never pretend to a purpose of its own; where, finally, bourgeois society itself, linking the productive forces of the old world with the gigantic natural terrain of the new, has developed to hitherto unknown dimensions and freedom of movement, and has far exceeded previous efforts to overcome the forces of nature, and where the contradictions of bourgeois society themselves appear only as transitory phenomena. It is not surprising that the production relationships in which this immense new world has developed so surprisingly quickly and fortunately are considered by Carey as the normal, eternal conditions of social production and distribution, contrary to what has taken place in Europe, especially in England – which for Carey is the real Europe – where the production relationships have been hindered and disturbed by the inherited obstacles of the feudal period. What more natural from his point of view, than that these relationships should have been caricatured and falsified by the English economists, who have confused the fortuitous distortions of these relationships with their inherent character?

Carey's criticism of the English theory of landed property, wages, population, class contradictions, etc., resolves itself into one thing only – American conditions against English conditions. Bourgeois society does not exist in the pure state in England; it does not there conform to its nature and definition. So why should the ideas of English economists on bourgeois society be the true and untroubled expression of a reality that they have never known? The disturbing effect on the natural relationships of bourgeois society amount, for Carey, in the last instance only to the influence of the state in its encroachments and interventions. It is a law of nature, for example, that wages should increase with the productivity of labour. So if reality does not correspond with this law, whether in India or in England, we have to make an abstraction of the influence of the state – taxes, monopolies, etc. Bourgeois conditions considered on their own, i.e. after discounting the influence of the state, will in fact always confirm the harmonious laws of bourgeois economy. Naturally, Carey does not inquire to what extent these state influences – public debt, taxes, etc. – themselves grow out of bourgeois conditions; thus in England, for example, they are not at all the result of feudalism, but rather of its dissolution and defeats, and in North America itself the power of the central government increases with the centralisation of capital.

While Carey urges the superiority of bourgeois society in North America as opposed to the English economists, Bastiat urges the inferiority of bourgeois society in France as opposed to the French socialists. You imagine, he says, that you can revolt against the laws of bourgeois society in a country in which these laws have never been allowed to take effect! You know these laws only in their stunted French form, and you assume their French caricature to be their natural form. But look across to England. Here bourgeois society has to be liberated from the chains imposed on it by the state. But you would like to multiply these chains. Aim first of all to promote pure bourgeois conditions, and then we will talk the matter over. (Bastiat is right, in as much as in France, because of its peculiar social organisation, a good deal passes for socialism which in England would be political economy.)

Carey, however, starting from the American emancipation of bourgeois society from the state, ends by postulating the interference of the state in bourgeois relations in order to safeguard the purity of their development, and not (as happened in fact in America) to be destroyed from outside. He is a Protectionist, while Bastiat is a Free Trader. On a world scale, the harmony of economic laws appears as a disharmony, and Carey is struck by the beginnings of this disharmony in the United States. Where does this strange phenomenon come from? Carey explains it by the destructive influence of England, whose aim is an industrial monopoly in the world market.

Originally, English conditions were perturbed internally by the false theories of their economists. But now, externally, England, as the dominant power in the world market, disturbs the harmony of economic conditions in all the countries of the world. This disharmony is a real thing, and does not merely arise from the subjective ideas of economists. What Russia is politically for Urquhart,[1] England is economically for Carey. According to Carey, the harmony of economic conditions is based on the harmonious co-operation of town and country, industry and agriculture. This fundamental harmony, which England has dissolved in her own land, is ruined as a result of her competition in world markets and is the destructive element in general harmony. The only possible protection against it is constituted by tariff barriers – a forcible, national barricade against the destructive force of British heavy industry. Thus the last refuge of economic harmony is the state, which originally was branded as the only element disturbing all this harmony.

Carey again describes here the particular national development of the United States, in opposition to and in competition with England. He does this in a naïve way, since he suggests that the United States should destroy the industrialism promoted by England, at the same time as developing it in the United States by means of tariff barriers. Apart from this naïvety, the harmony of bourgeois conditions of production ends for Carey with the most complete disharmony of these conditions when these appear on the greatest possible scale – in the world market – and in their

[1] [A frantically anti-Russian politician.]

most advanced development – in the relationships of producing nations. All relationships which seem harmonious to him when occurring within defined national frontiers or in their abstract form of the general relationships of bourgeois society – the concentration of capital, division of labour, the wage-earning class, etc. – appear to him discordant when they occur in their most developed form – the world market – for example, the internal relationships that produced British domination of the world market and that created the ruinous effects of this mastery. It is harmonious when, in any country, patriarchal production makes way for industrial production, and the process of dissolution that accompanies this development is only considered in its positive aspect. But it is disharmonious when British heavy industry dissolves the patriarchal or petit-bourgeois or any other backward forms of production of other nations! Carey sees only the positive side in the concentration of capital within a country and its dissolving influence. But the monopoly exercised by concentrated British capital, and its dissolving effect on the smaller national capitals of other countries is disharmonious. What Carey has not understood is that the disharmonies of the world market are only the ultimate and faithful reflection of disharmonies which have become fixed as abstract relations in economic categories or which exist locally on a reduced scale.

No wonder Carey forgets the positive aspect of this process of dissolution as it has developed fully in the world market, whereas he sees only the positive aspect of economic categories in their abstract form, or in the real conditions within countries whence these categories are drawn. This explains why his original optimism changes into an exacerbated and resentful pessimism when he comes up against economic conditions as they really are, in their universal reality. This contradiction is the key to the originality of his work, and affords it a certain significance. He is typically American both in his discovery of harmony within bourgeois society, and when he finds disharmony in those same conditions in the world market.

There is nothing of all this in Bastiat. For him, harmonious conditions start in the 'back of beyond' that begins after the French frontier has been passed – in England or America. It is simply an imaginary, idealised form of Anglo-American relations, of non-French relationships, not the real relationships that he might see within the boundaries of his own country. This is why, for him, harmony does not present a real living conception, but rather the flat and affected product of a thin, strained and contradictory reflection; the only element of reality that is found in him is when he calls upon the French state to open its economic frontiers. Carey sees the contradictions of economic conditions as soon as English conditions appear in the world market. Bastiat, for whom harmony arises only from his imagination, only begins to see its realisation where France comes to an end, and where the component parts of bourgeois society divided into nations are liberated from the supervision of the state and freely compete. This ultimate harmony – which is the precondition of all the other harmonies that he has imagined – is, however, no more than a postulate, to be realised by means of free trade legislation.

Thus Carey at least has the merit – apart from the scientific value of his work – that he expresses the important American relationships in an abstract form and in opposition to those of the old world; whereas the only real basis to be found in Bastiat is the pettiness of French conditions, which become transparent everywhere within his harmonies. However, his work is superfluous, for the conditions of such an old country are sufficiently known, and do not need to be described by such a negative detour. Carey is rich, so to speak, in bona-fide investigations into economic science, on credit, revenue, etc. Bastiat is only concerned with conciliatory paraphrases of researches that end in antagonism: hypocritical self-satisfaction. Carey's universality is that of the American. For him, France and China are equally close. He is always the man who lives on both the Atlantic and the Pacific Oceans. Bastiat's universality consists in making an abstraction of every country. Carey, a true Yankee, collects a quantity of material from all parts of the old world; it is not that he recognises the spirit inherent in all this material, thus conceding to it the right to a life of its own; he uses the material for his own purposes, as lifeless records, indifferent material that he can work over to prove theses inspired by his Yankee point of view. This is why he roams about everywhere, collecting masses of statistics quite uncritically, displaying his catalogue-like erudition.

Bastiat, on the other hand, loves imaginary history. He presents his abstractions sometimes in a reasoned form, and sometimes in the form of hypothetical events which have never taken place anywhere, just as a theologian considers sin sometimes as a law of human existence, and sometimes as the history of the fall of man into sin. Both are therefore unhistorical and anti-historical. But the absence of any historical element in Carey is the present historical principle of North America, whereas the unhistorical element in Bastiat is merely a throwback to the eighteenth-century fashion for generalisation in France. Thus Carey is shapeless and diffuse, while Bastiat is affected and formally logical. At best, Bastiat manages to formulate commonplaces, paradoxically expressed and with a polished façade. Carey expresses a few general ideas in the form of aphorisms, and following on this he advances as evidence a great mass of misshapen material which is merely a compilation and in no sense an elaboration of the content of his thesis. Apart from a few local examples, or normal English phenomena that he presents in a fantastic manner, the only material to be found in Bastiat consists in the general theories of economists. In short, the opposite of Carey is Ricardo, or the modern English economists; the opposite of Bastiat, the French socialists.

## WAGES

The following constitute Bastiat's main theses: all men strive to achieve a fixed income, or fixed revenue. (A truly French example: every man aspires to be a *fonctionnaire* or to make his son a *fonctionnaire*.) Wages constitute a fixed form of remuneration, and are thus a very perfected form of association, in the original form of which chance predominated, in so far as 'all the associates are subjected to all the hazards of the enterprise'.[1] From the moment when capital shoulders the risk on its own account, the remuneration of work is fixed under the name *wages*. If labour takes the responsibility for both good and bad consequences, the remuneration of capital becomes detached, and fixed under the name *interest*. However, if chance originally predominates in the condition of the worker, it is because stability is not yet adequately

[1] [This and the following quotations are from Bastiat's text.]

assured in the wage structure. It is an 'intermediate degree separating chance from stability'. This last stage is reached by 'saving, during working days, enough to meet one's needs when old or sick'. The last stage develops through 'mutual help societies' and in the last instance through 'the workers' retirement fund'. (Just as man began with the need to become a *fonctionnaire*, so he ends with the satisfaction of drawing his pension.)

1. Let us admit that everything Bastiat says about the fixity of wages is true. If we classify wages under fixed revenue, we are no nearer to understanding their real character, their peculiar characteristics. We have simply disengaged one of the facets that they have in common with other sources of income. Nothing more. This might be some use to the lawyer who had to argue a case in favour of the wage structure. But it is no use to the economist, who has to understand the peculiarity of this relationship in its entirety. To make a partial definition of a relationship or of an economic form, to make a panegyric of it against the opposite definition – this is the pedestrian lawyer's and apologist's practice that characterises Bastiat's reasoning. So put fixed income in place of wages. Is not a fixed income a good thing? Does not everyone like to calculate on something certain? Especially every mean-spirited Frenchman? *L'homme toujours besogneux?* It is in the same way, and perhaps with greater justification, that serfdom was defended. The opposite might be, and indeed has been, maintained. Suppose wages equal non-fixity, i.e. advancement beyond a certain point. Who does not like going forward instead of standing still? What is wrong with a relationship that offers the prospects of bourgeois progress *ad infinitum*? Bastiat himself in other passages naturally considers the wage structure as not being fixed. How else than through this non-fixity, through fluctuations of income, could the worker possibly cease working and become a capitalist, as Bastiat would like him to do? So the wage structure is a good thing, because it implies a fixed income; it is a good thing, because it implies the absence of fixity; it is a good thing, because it is neither one thing nor the other, yet it is both at the same time. Which relationship is not good, if considered from a single aspect which is judged positively and not negatively? All this sagacious blather, all this apologia and philistine sophistry rests on abstractions of this kind.

After these preliminary remarks, we come to Bastiat's really constructive ideas. (It might be said in passing that the tenant farmer of the French countryside, the man in whom the misery of the wage-earner is united with the bad fortune of the petty capitalist, might indeed count himself lucky if he were on a fixed wage. Proudhon's *Histoire descriptive et philosophique* is scarcely on the same level as that of his opponent Bastiat. There follows on the primitive form of association, in which all the associates share the risks, a higher stage of association, entered into voluntarily by both sides, in which the remuneration of the worker is fixed. We do not want to stress here the ingenuity that presupposes the capitalist at one pole and the worker at the other, and then develops, by mutual agreement, the relationship between capital and wage-labour.)

The form of the association in which the worker is exposed to all the accidental chances of earning a living – in which all producers are equally exposed to such risks – and which immediately precedes wages, in which the remuneration of labour achieves fixity and stability, just as a thesis precedes its antithesis, is, according to Bastiat, the state of society wherein hunting, fishing and cattle-raising make up the dominant forms of production and society. First of all the nomadic fisherman, huntsman or cowherd – and then the wage-earner. Where and when did this historical transformation occur from the half-savage state to the modern world? In the *Charivari*,[1] perhaps! In real history, wage-labour appears when slavery and bondage disappear – or when communal property falls into disuse, as with oriental and Slav peoples. In its developed, epoch-making form, that in which it embraces the whole social essence of labour, it arises from the ruins of the guild economy, the system of estates, natural labour and natural income, industry practised as a rural accessory, and feudal small-scale agriculture, etc. In all these real historical phases of transition, wage-labour dissolves and destroys the relationships in which labour was fixed as regards its revenue, content, place, quantity, etc. In fact, it became *the negation of any fixity of labour and remuneration*. The direct transition from the African fetish to Voltaire's *Être Suprême* or from the bows and arrows of a primitive Red Indian to the capital of the Bank of England, is not so

[1] [A contemporary French satirical journal.]

absurdly contrary to historical fact as the transition of Bastiat's fisherman to the wage-earner. (In all this series of evolutions, moreover, there is no sign of changes arising from voluntary and mutual agreement.) Of the same value as the historical construction built up by Bastiat – in which he deceives himself into thinking of his superficial abstractions as actual facts – is his synthesis which sets up the English friendly societies and savings banks as the last word in the wage structure, and as the abolition of all social contradictions.

Thus, historically, the non-fixed character of wages is the contrary of Bastiat's construction. But how was it that he arrived at the construction of fixity as the definition of the wage structure that compensates for everything else? And how did he come to want to show the wage structure historically in this definition, as the highest form of the remuneration of labour in other forms of society and association?

When it is a question of the given relationship between capital and wage-labour, between profit and wages, all economists wish to demonstrate to the worker that he has no claim to participate in the possibilities of profit, and they try to reassure him concerning his subordinate role vis-à-vis the capitalist. They point out that, contrary to the capitalist, the worker benefits from a certain stability of income, which is more or less independent of the great adventures of capital. In just the same way, Don Quixote consoled Sancho Panza: certainly he had to take all the blows, but he had no need to be courageous. While the economists apply this idea to profit, as opposed to wages, Bastiat makes of it an inherent quality of wages as opposed to the earlier forms of labour, presenting it as progress in relation to remuneration of labour in these earlier forms. Thus Mr Bastiat extracts from the relationship between capital and labour a platitude designed to console the worker vis-à-vis the capitalist, and makes of this platitude, torn from its context, the historical foundation of this relationship. In the relations of wages to profit, and of wage-labour to capital, say the economists, wages have the advantage of stability. But Mr Bastiat says that fixity, i.e. one of the aspects of the wages–profit relation, is the historical basis for the coming into being not only of wages (or, fixity is the attribute of wages in opposition not to profit, but to the earlier forms of remuneration of labour) but also of profit, that is, the whole relationship. In this way a commonplace referring to one aspect of the relationship between wages and profit becomes surreptitiously transformed into the historical cause of the whole relationship. Bastiat proceeds in this way because he is constantly preoccupied with the thought of socialism, imagined by him everywhere to be the first form of association. This example shows the importance assumed in Bastiat's hands by the polemical platitudes which in economic theory occupy only a secondary place.

To return to the economists. What does this fixity of wages consist in? Are wages unalterably fixed? This would flatly contradict the law of supply and demand, the basis of the fixing of wages. No economist has denied that wages fluctuate, that they rise and fall. Or are wages independent of crises? Or of machines, which make wage-labour superfluous? Or of the divisions of labour, which displace it? It would be heterodox to maintain this, and no one has done so. What is meant is that an average wage level is attained in a defined cross-section of wage-labour, i.e. that, for the class as a whole, the minimum wage so odious to Bastiat in fact exists, and a definite average continuity of labour occurs, so that, for example, wages could continue even in cases where profit momentarily decreased or even disappeared. What can this mean, if not that, assuming wage-labour to be the dominant form of labour and the foundation of production, the working class lives from its wages, and individual labour possesses, on average, the fixity of being of the wage-earning type? In other words, this is a tautology. Whenever the dominant relationship of production consists of capital and wage-labour, there is continuity of wage-labour, in so far as there is a fixed wage for the worker. Wherever wage-labour exists, it exists. And this is what Bastiat considers its universally compensating property! Moreover, that as capital develops, society and social production become in general more regular, more continuous and more universal – while the income of those participating in it becomes more fixed – than in a situation where capital and its production have not yet developed to this stage, is again a tautology, inherent in the concept of capital and of the production founded on it. In other words: who would deny that the universal existence of wage-labour presumes a higher development of productivity than in the stages preceding wage-labour? How could it occur to the socialists to raise their demands, did they not presuppose the superior development of social productivity brought forth by wage-labour? The latter is rather the precondition of their claim.

*Note*: The first general form of wage-labour was soldiers' pay, occurring as national armies and bourgeois militia declined. First of all the bourgeois themselves received the pay. Then their place was taken by mercenaries who had ceased to be bourgeois.

2. (It is impossible to pursue this nonsense any further. We therefore drop Mr Bastiat.)

# 3 Money as a Symbol of Alienation in Capitalist Society

From *Grundrisse*, pp. 63–7

*Marx here describes the alienation that, in his view, necessarily arises when the exchange of goods in society is effected by money equivalents.*

THE process is thus simply that the product becomes a commodity, that is, *a pure element of exchange*. Commodities are converted into exchange value. So that it can be identified as exchange value, it is exchanged for a symbol, which represents it as exchange value properly so called. In this symbolic form it can again be exchanged, under certain conditions, for any other goods. When the product becomes a commodity, and the commodity becomes exchange value, it possesses (ideally at first) a double existence. This ideal dual identity necessarily means that the commodity appears in a dual form when actually exchanged: as a natural product on the one hand, as an exchange value on the other. In other words, its exchange value has a material existence, apart from the product.

The definition of the product as exchange value necessarily entails that the exchange value leads a separate existence, severed from the product. This exchange value which is severed from the commodity and yet is itself a commodity is – *money*. All the properties of the commodity viewed as exchange value appear as an object distinct from it; they exist in the social form of money, quite separate from their natural form of existence.

(The material in which this symbol is expressed is not at all a matter of indifference, however diverse it may have appeared during the course of history. The development of society has involved the repeated elaboration of this symbol – and the material that best expresses it – which it has in turn continually rejected. If a symbol is not to be an arbitrary one, it requires that the material of which it is made should fulfil certain conditions. Thus the symbols for words have a history, form an alphabet, etc.)

The exchange value of the product thus creates money alongside the product. It is impossible to abolish the implications and contradictions that result from the existence of money alongside particular commodities by simply altering the form of money (although it is possible to avoid the difficulties inherent in a lower form of money by using a higher form); and it is equally impossible to abolish money altogether, so long as exchange value remains the social form of products. It is important to understand this clearly in order to avoid setting oneself impossible tasks, and it is also important to grasp the limits within which the relations of production and the social relationships that depend upon them can be reconstructed by reforms of money and circulation.

The properties of money are: (1) a standard for the measurement of the exchange of commodities; (2) means of exchange; (3) representative of commodities (and thus the object of a contract); (4) as a universal commodity alongside special kinds of commodity. All these properties arise from the definition of money as the exchange value of commodities, severed from them and having its own objectified existence.

(The nature of money as the universal commodity with regard to all others, as the incarnation of their exchange value, has led to its being the realised – and permanently realisable – form of capital, a form in which capital may constantly and validly appear. This property is manifested, for example, in the 'bullion drain'. This means that, from the historical point of view, capital originally appeared only in the form of money; and this explains the close connection of money with interest rates and its influence on them.)

The more production is shaped in such a way that every producer depends on the exchange value of his commodities, i.e. the more the product really becomes an exchange value, and exchange value becomes the direct object of production, the more must *money relationships* develop, as also the contradictions inherent in this money relationship, in the relation of the product to itself as money.

The necessity of exchange and the transformation of the product into a pure exchange value progress to the same extent as the division of labour, i.e. with the social character of production. But just as exchange value grows, the power of money grows too; that is, the exchange relationship establishes itself as a force externally opposed to the producers, and independent of them. What was originally a means to the furtherance of production becomes a relationship alien to the producers. The more the producers become dependent upon exchange, the more exchange seems to be independent of them; and the gap between the product as a product and the product as an exchange value widens.

Money does not generate these antagonisms and contradictions; but their development generates the seemingly transcendental power of money. (We shall have to analyse in detail the effect of the transformation of all relations into money relations: natural taxes becoming money taxes, natural income becoming money income, military service becoming the engagement of mercenaries, and especially all personal services taking on a monetary nature, and patriarchal, servile, bonded and guild labour changing into pure wage-labour.)

The product becomes a commodity; the commodity becomes exchange value; the exchange value of commodities is their inherent monetary property; and this monetary property is severed from them in the form of money, and achieves a social existence apart from all particular commodities and their natural mode of existence. The relation of the product to itself as an exchange value becomes its relation to money existing alongside it, or of all products to the money that exists outside them all. Just as the actual exchange of products creates their exchange value, so their exchange value creates money.

The next question that confronts us is: does not the existence of money alongside commodities conceal from the outset contradictions that are implicit in this relationship?

1. Commodities exist in a double form: first, as a definite product that ideally contains (in latent form) its exchange value in its natural form of existence; second, as the exchange value made evident (money), which has given up all contact with the natural form of existence of the product. This simple fact means that these two separate existences must lead to a *difference*, and the difference will lead to antagonism and contradiction.

The same contradiction between the particular nature of the

commodity considered as a product and its universal nature as an exchange value which created the need for it to exist in a double form, first of all as a particular commodity, then as money – this contradiction between its special natural properties and its universal social properties implies from the start the possibility that both these separated forms of existence of the commodity are not interconvertible. The exchangeability of commodities exists as a material thing alongside them in the form of money, as something different from them and no longer directly identical. As soon as money becomes an external thing alongside commodities, the exchangeability of commodities for money is immediately attached to external conditions which may or may not occur; it is the victim of external conditions. In the exchange, goods are required for their natural properties, depending on the needs that they satisfy. Money, on the other hand, is only required for its exchange value. Whether commodities are to be exchanged for money, and, therefore, whether an exchange value can be set for the goods will be decided by circumstances which have nothing to do with the exchange value and are independent of it. The exchangeability of commodities depends on the natural properties of the product; that of money coincides with its existence as a symbolic exchange value. It is thus possible that commodities, in their particular form as products, cannot be exchanged or converted into the universal form of money. In view of its external existence as money, the exchangeability of commodities is different from them and has become alien to them: it is initially unequal to them, and must be made equal. But this return to equality is dependent on other conditions, i.e. on chance.

2. Just as exchange value leads a double existence, as particular commodities and as money, so the act of exchange splits into two acts that are independent of one another: exchange of commodities for money, exchange of money for commodities – buying and selling. There is no longer any immediate identity, since they have been separated in time and space, each one having acquired a form of existence which is indifferent to the other. They may or may not coincide or meet; they may be in disproportion to one another. There will certainly be constant attempts to make them tally; but in place of the previous immediate equality, there is now a constant movement towards equality, implying a continual

inequality. Harmony can no longer be obtained except through allowing the most extreme disharmonies to run their course.

3. The separation between buying and selling, the splitting of exchange into two acts, independent of each other spatially and temporally, brings a new relation into being.

At the same time that exchange is thus divided into two mutually independent acts, the entire process of exchange is separated from those exchanging, the producers of the commodities. Exchange for its own sake is separated from exchange for the sake of goods. A class of traders appears between the producers, a class of men who only buy in order to sell, and only sell in order to buy once more, their purpose being not to acquire the goods as products, but only to retain the exchange values themselves, that is, the money. (A trader class can also appear simply in the exchange of goods. But since such traders only have at their disposal the surplus production from both sides, their influence on production is entirely secondary, and so is their importance.)

When exchange value adopts an autonomous form as money, by being detached from the products, there occurs a corresponding autonomy of exchange (trade) as a function detached from the exchangers. Exchange value was the standard by which goods were exchanged, but its purpose was the direct possession of the exchanged goods, and consumption of them (either to satisfy needs directly, by making use of the product, or in order to make the instruments of production).

The immediate purpose of trade is not consumption, but the amassing of money, of exchange values. As a result of this doubling of exchange – exchange for the sake of consumption and exchange for its own sake – a new incongruity arises. The trader as he makes his exchange is only concerned with the difference between the buying and the selling price of goods; but the consumer has to replace definitively the exchange value of the goods that he buys. Although there is a certain reciprocity in the end between circulation or exchange among traders and the end of circulation, or exchange between traders and consumers, these are determined by quite different laws and motives, and may come into violent contradiction with one another.

We already see in this separation the possibility of trade crises. Since production, however, works directly for trade and only indirectly for consumption, it too must be affected by the disproportion between trade and exchange for consumption that it itself produces. (The relation between supply and demand is completely inverted.) (Trade in money then again becomes detached from trade *per se*.)

# 4 Social Power and the Individual

From *Grundrisse*, pp. 73–7

*Marx here describes the isolated position of the alienated individual in a society where all exchange is mediated through money.*

THE disintegration of all products and activities into exchange values presupposes both the disintegration of all rigid, personal (historical) relationships of dependence in production, and a universal interdependence of the producers. The production of each individual depends on everyone else's production, just as the transformation of his product into food for himself depends on everyone else's consumption. Prices are ancient; and so is exchange; but the increasing determination of prices by the cost of production, and the influence of exchange over all production relationships can only develop fully and ever more completely in bourgeois society, the society of free competition. What Adam Smith, in true eighteenth-century style, places in the prehistoric period, puts before history, is in fact its product.

This mutual dependence is expressed in the constant need for exchange, value being the universal intermediary. The economists express it like this: each person has his private interests in mind, and nothing else; as a consequence he serves everyone's private interests, i.e. the general interest, without wishing to or knowing that he is. The irony of this is not that the totality of private interest – which is the same thing as the general interest – can be attained by the individual's following his own interest. Rather it could be inferred from this abstract phrase that everyone hinders the satisfaction of everyone else's interest, that instead of a general affirmation, the result of this war of all against all is rather a general negation. The point is rather that private interest is itself already a socially determined interest, which can only be achieved within the conditions established by society and through the means that society affords, and that it is thus linked to the reproduction of these conditions and means. It is certainly the interest of private individuals that is at stake; but its content, as well as the form and the means of its realisation, is only given by social conditions independent of all these individuals.

The mutual and universal dependence of individuals who remain indifferent to one another constitutes the social network that binds them together. This social coherence is expressed in *exchange value*, in which alone each individual's activity or his product becomes an activity or a product for him. He has to produce a general product: *exchange value* or – in its isolated, individualised form – *money*. On the other hand the power that each individual exercises over others' activity or over social wealth exists in him as the owner of exchange values, money. Thus both his power over society and his association with it is carried in his pocket. Whatever the individual form in which activity occurs, and whatever the particular characteristics of the product of activity, they are *exchange value*, that is, a general factor in which all individuality and particularity is denied and suppressed. This is in effect a very different set of circumstances from that in which the individual, or the individual spontaneously and historically enlarged into the family and the tribe (and later the community), reproduces himself directly from nature, or his productive activity and his share in the production are dependent on a particular form of labour and of product, and his relationship to others is likewise determined.

The social character of activity, and the social form of the product, as well as the share of the individual in production, are here opposed to individuals as something alien and material; this does not consist in the behaviour of some to others, but in their subordination to relations that exist independently of them and arise from the collision of indifferent individuals with one another. The general exchange of activities and products, which has become a condition of living for each individual and the link between them, seems to them to be something alien and independent, like a thing.

In exchange value, the social relations of individuals have become transformed into the social connections of material things; personal power has changed into material power. The less social power the means of exchange possess and the closer they are still connected with the nature of the direct product of labour and the immediate needs of those exchanging, the greater must be the power of the community to bind the individuals together: the patriarchal relationship, the ancient communities, feudalism and the guild system. Each individual possesses social power in the form of a material object. If the object is deprived of its social power then this power must be exercised by people over people.

Relationships of personal dependence (which were at first quite spontaneous) are the first forms of society in which human productivity develops, though only to a slight extent and at isolated points. Personal independence founded on *material* dependence is the second great form: in it there developed for the first time a system of general social interchange, resulting in universal relations, varied requirements and universal capacities. Free individuality, which is founded on the universal development of individuals and the domination of their communal and social productivity, which has become their social power, is the third stage. The second stage creates the conditions for the third. Patriarchal and ancient societies (feudal also) decline as trade, luxury, money and exchange value develop, just as modern society has grown up simultaneously alongside these.

Exchange and the division of labour mutually condition one another. Given that everyone works for himself but that his product is not created for himself, he must of course exchange it, not only in order to obtain a share in general productive capacity, but in order to transform his own production into means of subsistence for himself. Exchange, negotiated through exchange value and money, implies a universal interdependence between the producers, but at the same time the complete isolation of their private interests and a division of social labour, whose unity and mutual fulfilment exists as an external, natural relationship, independent of the individuals. The tension between universal supply and demand constitutes the social network that binds the indifferent individuals together.

The very necessity of first transforming the product or the activity of the individuals into the form of *exchange value* or *money*, that they acquire and demonstrate their social power only in this material form, shows both that: (1) the individuals are now producing only in and for society; and (2) that their production is not directly social, not the offspring of an association that divides the labour among its members. The individuals are subordinated to social production, which exists externally to them, as a sort of fate; but social production is not subordinated to the individuals who manipulate it as their communal capacity.

Nothing, therefore, could be more incorrect and absurd than to presume, on the basis of exchange value and money, the control of associated individuals over their general production as occurred above with the bank issuing vouchers for hours of work.

The *private exchange* of all the products of labour, capacities and activities is opposed to the distribution founded on the spontaneous or political hierarchy of individuals within patriarchal, ancient or feudal societies (where exchange only plays a secondary role and hardly affects the entire life of communities, since it only occurs between them and does not dominate all the relationships of production and commerce). But private exchange is opposed just as much to the free exchange of associated individuals on the basis of collective appropriation and control of the means of production. (This last association is not arbitrary: it presupposes the development of material and intellectual conditions which cannot be discussed here.)

The division of labour results in concentration, co-ordination, co-operation, the antagonism of private interests and class interests, competition, the centralisation of capital, monopolies and joint stock companies – so many contradictory forms of unity which in turn engenders all these contradictions. In the same way private exchange creates world trade, private independence gives rise to complete dependence on the so-called world market, and the fragmented acts of exchange make a system of banks and credit necessary, whose accounts at least settle the balances of private exchange. National trade acquires a semblance of existence in the foreign exchange market – although the private interests within each nation divide them into as many nations as they possess full-grown individuals, and the interests of exporters and importers of the same nation are here opposed. No one would imagine that it was therefore possible to transform the foundations of internal and external trade by means of stock exchange reform. But within bourgeois society, which is founded on exchange value, relationships of commerce and production develop which are so many mines about to explode beneath them.

(There exist innumerable contradictory forms of social unity whose contradictory character can never be exploded by peaceful metamorphosis. On the other hand, all our attempts to explode them would be merely quixotic, if we could not find embedded in society as it is today the material conditions of production and the commercial relationships of the classless society.) . . . It need only be further remarked here that a survey of trade in general and production in general, so far as it actually exists in the lists of market prices, furnishes in fact the best evidence as to how their own exchange and their own production stands in opposition to individuals as a thing-like relationship which is *independent of them*. In the *world market*, the *connection of the individual* with the whole – but also, and simultaneously *the independence of this connection from the individuals* – has itself progressed to such a level that its formation already itself embodies the precondition for its becoming something different. A parallel can be drawn with the position of genuine common interest and universality.

# 5 Alienation, Social Relationships and Free Individuality

From *Grundrisse*, pp. 80–2

*Marx contrasts the social relationships in the feudal and bourgeois epochs, the former being characterised by relationships that were personal as against the purely material relationships of the latter. Marx then asks whether freedom was increased by this transition.*

IT has been said, and bears repeating, that the beauty and grandeur of the system is founded on this connection and on this material and spiritual interchange, which is spontaneous, independent of the knowledge and desires of the individual, and in fact requires their indifference to each other and mutual independence. Certainly this connection by means of things is to be preferred to a lack of connection, or a merely local association which is founded on a relationship consisting of blood ties, or one of supremacy or servitude; and it is just as certain that individuals cannot dominate their own social relationships until they have created them. But it is absurd to interpret these *purely material* relationships as natural relationships, inseparable from the nature of individuality (in contrast to reflected knowledge and desire) and inherent in it. These relationships are produced by individuals, produced historically. They belong to a definite phase of the development of the individual. The heterogeneity and independence in which these relationships still stand opposed to individuals, prove only that these individuals are still engaged in the production of the conditions of their social life, rather than that they began that life starting from those conditions. This is the natural and spontaneous interrelationship of individuals inside production relations that are determined and narrowly limited. Universally developed individuals, whose social relationships are subject, as their own communal relationships, to their own collective control, are the product not of nature but of history. The extent and universality of the development of capacities which make possible this sort of individuality, presupposes precisely production on the basis of exchange values. The universal nature of this production creates an alienation of the individual from himself and others, but also for the first time the general and universal nature of his relationships and capacities. At early stages of development the single individual appears to be more complete, since he has not yet elaborated the abundance of his relationships, and has not established them as powers and autonomous social relationships that are opposed to himself. It is as ridiculous to wish to return to that primitive abundance as it is to believe in the continuing necessity of its complete depletion. The bourgeois view has never got beyond opposition to this romantic outlook and thus will be accompanied by it, as a legitimate antithesis, right up to its blessed end.

(To compare money with blood – as suggested by the word 'circulation' – is just about as apt as Menenius Agrippa's comparison between the patricians and the stomach. It is no less false to compare money with language. It is not the case that ideas are transmuted in language in such a way that their particular nature disappears and their social character exists alongside them in language, as prices exist alongside goods. Ideas do not exist apart from language. Ideas that have first to be translated from their native language into a foreign language in order to circulate, in order to be exchangeable, constitute a slightly closer analogy; but the analogy here lies not in the language, but in their being in a *foreign* language.)

(The exchangeability of all products, activities and relationships against a third, or *material*, factor, which can again be exchanged against everything else *without exception* – in other words the development of exchange values (and money relationships) is the same thing as general venality and corruption. Universal prostitution appears as a necessary phase of the development of the social character of personal talents, abilities, capacities and activities. This could be more delicately expressed as the general condition of serviceability and usefulness. It is the bringing to a common level of different things, which is the significance that already Shakespeare gave to money. Addiction to wealth as such is impossible without money; all other forms of accumulation, and addiction to them, appear as primitive, limited and conditioned by needs on the one hand, and by the narrowly limited nature of the products on the other (*sacra auri fames*).)

(The money system in its development obviously presupposes other general developments.)

When social conditions are considered that generate an undeveloped system of exchange, exchange values and money, or to which an undeveloped stage of such a system corresponds, it is immediately evident that the individuals, although their relationships appear to be more personal, only relate to each other in determined roles, as a feudal lord and his vassal, a landlord and his serf, etc., or as a member of a caste, etc., or of an estate, etc. In money relationships, in the developed exchange system (and it is this semblance that is so seductive in the eyes of democrats), the ties of personal dependence are in fact broken, torn asunder, as also differences of blood, educational differences, etc. (the personal ties all appear at least to be *personal* relationships). Thus the individuals appear to be independent (though this independence is merely a complete illusion and should rather be termed indifference); independent, that is, to collide with one another freely and to barter within the limits of this freedom. They appear so, however, only to someone who abstracts from the conditions of existence in which these individuals come into contact. (Such conditions are again independent of individuals and appear, although they were created by society, to be the same as *natural conditions*, i.e. uncontrollable by the individual.) The determining factor that appears in the first case to be a personal limitation of one individual by another, seems in the latter to be built up into a material limitation of the individual by circumstances that are independent of him and self-contained. (Since the single individual cannot shed his personal limitations, but can surmount external circumstances and master them, his freedom *appears* to be greater in the second case. Closer investigation of these external circumstances and conditions shows, however, how impossible it is for the individuals forming part of a class, etc., to surmount them *en masse* without abolishing them. The individual may by chance be rid of them; but not the masses that are ruled by them, since their mere existence is an expression of the subordination to which individuals must necessarily submit.) So far from constituting the removal of a 'state of dependence', these external relationships represent its disintegration into a general form; or better: they are the elaboration of the general *basis* of personal states of dependence. Here too individuals come into relation with one another only in a determined role. These material states of dependence, as opposed to the personal states, are also characterised by the fact that individuals are now controlled only by abstractions, whereas earlier they depended on one another. (The material state of dependence is no more than autonomous social relationships opposed to apparently independent individuals, i.e. their mutual relations of production, which have become independent, in opposition to them.) This abstraction or idea is merely the theoretical expression of the material relationships that dominate individuals. Relationships, of course, can be expressed only in ideas, so that philosophers have construed as the chief characteristic of modern times the fact that they are dominated by ideas and have identified the genesis of free individuality with the fall of this domination of ideas. It was all the easier to commit this error from the ideological point of view, since this domination of relationships (that material dependence which moreover once more changes into determined personal states of dependence, but divested of all illusion) itself appears in the consciousness of individuals as a domination of ideas, and since the belief in the eternity of these ideas, i.e. of these material states of dependence, is, of course, in every way confirmed, nourished and inculcated by the ruling classes.

(Of course as for the illusion of the 'purely personal relationships' of feudal times, etc., one must never forget for a moment that: (1) these circumstances themselves took on a material character at a certain stage within their own sphere, as shown, for example, in the development of landed property relationships from purely military states of subordination; but (2) the material relationships to which they give way have themselves a narrowly limited character, determined by nature, and thus *appear* to be personal, whereas in the modern world personal relationships occur purely as a result of relationships of production and exchange.)

# 6 General and Specific Labour

From *Grundrisse*, pp. 88–90

*Marx gives here an account of the universal nature of labour in the future communist society. The passage at the end is probably the fullest account in Marx of the nature of labour in the future communist society and complements his description in the* Critique of the Gotha Programme.

CONSIDERED in the act of production itself, the labour of the individual is used by him as money to buy the product directly, that is, the object of his own activity; but it is particular money, used to buy this particular product. In order to be money in general, it must originate from general and not special labour; that is, it must originally be established as an element of general production. But on this presupposition it is not basically exchange that gives it its general character, but its presupposed social character will determine its participation in the products. The social character of production would make the product from the start a collective and general product. The exchange originally found in production – which is an exchange not of exchange values but of activities determined by communal needs and communal aims – would from the start imply the participation of individuals in the collective world of products.

On the basis of exchange values, it is exchange that first makes of labour something general. In the other system labour is established as such before the exchange; that is, the exchange of products is not at all the medium by which participation of the individual in general production is brought about. There must of course be mediation. In the first case, we start with the autonomous production of private individuals (however much it is determined and modified subsequently by complex relationships) and mediation is carried out by the exchange of goods, exchange value and money, which are all expressions of one and the same relationship. In the second case, the presupposition itself is mediated, i.e. the precondition is collective production; the community is the foundation of production. The labour of the individual is established from the start as collective labour. But whatever the particular form of the product which he creates or helps to create, what he has bought with his labour is not this or that product, but a definite participation in collective production. Therefore he has no special product to exchange. His product is not an exchange value. The product does not have to change into any special form in order to have a general character for the individual. Instead of a division of labour necessarily engendered by the exchange of values, there is an organisation of labour, which has as its consequence the participation of the individual in collective consumption.

In the first case, the social character of production is established subsequently by the elevation of products to exchange values, and the exchange of these values. In the second case, the social character of production is a precondition, and participation in the world of production and in consumption is not brought about by the exchange of labour or the products of labour which are independent of it. It is brought about by the social conditions of production, within which the individual acts.

Thus the desire to turn individual labour directly into money (which also includes the product of labour), i.e. into a realised exchange value, means that the worker's labour must be designated as general labour. In other words, this means that those conditions are denied in which he must necessarily become money and exchange value, and is dependent on private exchange. This requirement can be satisfied only in conditions in which it is no longer set. On the basis of exchange values, neither the labour of the individual nor his product are directly general; to obtain this character, an objective mediation is required, money distinct from the product.

If we suppose communal production, the determination of time remains, of course, essential. The less time society requires in order to produce wheat, cattle, etc., the more time it gains for other forms of production, material or intellectual. As with a single individual, the universality of its development, its enjoyment and its activity depends on saving time. In the final analysis, all forms of economics can be reduced to an economics of time. Likewise, society must divide up its time purposefully in order to achieve a production suited to its general needs; just as the individual has to divide his time in order to acquire, in suitable proportions, the knowledge he needs or to fulfil the various requirements of his activity.

On the basis of community production, the first economic law thus remains the economy of time, and the methodical distribution of working time between the various branches of production; and this law becomes indeed of much greater importance. But all this differs basically from the measurement of exchange values (labour and the products of labour) by labour time. The work of individuals participating in the same branch of activity, and the different kinds of labour are not only quantitatively but also qualitatively different. What is the precondition of a merely quantitative difference between things? The fact that their quality is the same. Thus units of labour can be measured quantitatively only if they are of equal and identical quality.

# 7 Individuals and Society

From *Grundrisse*, pp. 175–6

*Marx analyses society as the sum of relationships between individuals, and individuals as mediated through society.*

NOTHING is more false than the way in which society has been treated both by economists and by socialists in relation to economic conditions. For example Proudhon says, against Bastiat (XVI 29): 'There is no difference, *for society*, between capital and product. This difference is a purely *subjective* one dependent upon the individual.' Thus he calls precisely the social *subjective*; and he terms the subjective abstraction *society*. The difference between product and capital is precisely that the product, as capital, expresses a distinct relationship belonging to a historical form of society. The so-called 'consideration from the standpoint of society' means only the overlooking of precisely those *differences* which express the *social relationships* (the relationship of bourgeois society). Society does not consist of individuals; it expresses the sum of connections and relationships in which individuals find themselves. It is as though one were to say: from the standpoint of society there are neither slaves nor citizens: both are men. Rather they are so *outside* society. To be a slave or to be a citizen are social determinations, the relationships of Man A and Man B. Man A is not a slave as such. He is a slave within society and because of it. What Mr Proudhon says here concerning capital and product means that, to him, from the standpoint of society there is no difference between capitalists and workers; whereas this is a difference that exists in fact only from the point of view of society.)

# 8 Capital and Labour as Productive and Unproductive

From *Grundrisse*, pp. 211–17

*The following passage begins with a rather obscure discussion of capital as a productive process and goes on to discuss whether capital or labour is the basic element in the productive process. It ends with an account of how the productivity of the worker contributes to his alienation.*

NOTHING can result at the end of a process that did not occur at its beginning as a prerequisite and condition. On the other hand, however, the result must contain all the elements of the process. Therefore if capital appears to have disappeared as a form of relationship at the end of the production process that was begun with capital as a prerequisite, this can only happen because we have overlooked the invisible threads that are drawn through this process by capital. So let us consider this aspect of the matter.

In the first place we find:

Through the incorporation of labour within capital, capital becomes a production process; but in the first place a *material* production process; a production process generally speaking, so that the production process of capital is not differentiated from the material production process generally speaking. The determination of its form has been completely extinguished. Because capital has exchanged part of its objective existence against labour, its objective existence is in itself divided into object and labour; the production process or, more exactly, the labour process, is formed by the connection between the two.

The labour process, which antedates value and serves as its starting point, thus again makes its appearance *within capital*, as a process which occurs inside its substance and forms its content. The labour process, because of its abstractness and its material nature, is equally characteristic of all forms of production.

(It will be shown that within this production process itself, this extinction of the determined form is only apparent.)

In so far as capital is value, but appears as a process in the first place in the form of a simple production process – a production process which cannot be limited as such to any special economic category, but only as a production process generally speaking – so it can be said that capital becomes a product, or is an instrument of labour, or even the raw material of labour. Any special aspect, as the case may be, of the simple production process, can be attached to it and this process, as we have seen, does not as such require capital at all, but is characteristic of all kinds of production. If it is, further, again understood as one of the features that contrast with labour as material, or merely as a means, then we can truly say that capital is not productive,[1] since it is then

---

[1] A point that has been much discussed, ever since Adam Smith made the distinction, concerns what productive labour is, or is not; the answer must follow from the analysis of the various aspects of capital. Productive labour is simply labour that produces capital. Is it not absurd, asks Mr Senior, for example (at least something like this), that the piano-maker is regarded as a productive worker, but not the pianist, although without the pianist the piano would have no meaning? But this is exactly the position. The piano-maker reproduces capital; the pianist merely exchanges his labour for income. But the pianist produces music and satisfies our musical sense; perhaps to some extent he produces this sense. In fact he does this: his work does produce something, but it is not therefore productive labour in the economic sense, any more than the work of a madman is productive when he produces hallucinations. Labour is only productive so long as it is producing its antithesis. Other economists allow that the so-called unproductive worker is indirectly productive. For example, the pianist stimulates production, either in that he raises our individuality to a more active, livelier level, or in the more usual sense, in that he arouses a fresh demand, in the fulfilment of which greater pains are taken with directly material production. It is already admitted here that only labour that produces capital is productive; so that labour which does not do this, however useful it may be (it could be harmful) is not productive for capitalisation, and hence is unproductive work. Other economists say that the difference between productive and unproductive cannot refer to production, but only to consumption. Quite the contrary. The tobacco producer is productive, although tobacco consumption is unproductive. Production for unproductive consumption is quite as productive as that for productive consumption; always supposing that it produces or reproduces capital. 'A productive labourer [is one who] directly augments his master's wealth', says Malthus quite correctly (ix 40); at least this is correct from one angle. The expression is too abstract, since in this wording it also applies to slaves. His

considered to be only the object that opposes labour, as something merely passive. The truth of the matter is, however, that it occurs not as one of the features, or as the difference between one aspect and it itself, nor as a mere result (product), but as the simple production process itself; that this process occurs as the self-moving content of capital.

Now to consider the aspect of the definition of form, as it is contained and modified in the production process.

As use value, labour exists only for capital, and is the use value of capital itself, i.e. the intermediary through which it turns itself into value. Capital, when it reproduces and increases its value, is the self-supporting exchange value (money) as a process, the process of valorisation. Hence, labour has no use value for the worker; hence, labour does not exist for him as the productive force of wealth, as the means or the activity of enrichment. The worker contributes labour as use value to be exchanged against capital, which is opposed to him not as capital but as money. It is capital, as capital, only in relation to the worker through the consumption of his labour, which initially remains outside this exchange and is independent of it. Although work is use value for capital, it only has exchange value for the worker; tangible exchange value. It is established as such in the act of exchange with capital, when it is sold for money. The use value of any object does not concern the seller as such, only the buyer of it. The property of saltpetre, that it can be used in the form of gun powder, does not determine the price of saltpetre; this price is determined rather by the production costs of saltpetre itself, the amount of work objectified in it. In the course of circulation, during which use value becomes cash in the form of prices, its value does not result from the circulation, even though it was realised solely there; it is a prerequisite of circulation, and only becomes translated into reality when exchanged against money. Thus labour, which has been sold by the worker to capital as *use value*, is the worker's *exchange value*, which he wishes to translate into reality, but is already *determined* before the act of exchange as a precondition imposed upon the worker. It is determined, as

master's wealth, in relation to the worker, is the form of wealth itself in relationship to work, i.e. capital. A productive labourer is one who directly augments capital. [Footnote by Marx.]

is the value of any other goods, by supply and demand; or in general, and this is the only aspect that concerns us here, by production costs, by the amount of work objectified in it, through which the worker's ability to work is produced, and which he therefore obtains as an equivalent. The exchange value of work, which is realised in the exchange process with the capitalist, is thus presupposed and predetermined, and it suffers only the formal modification that any ideally fixed price undergoes when it is realised. It is not determined by the use value of the work. For the worker himself, it only possesses use value in so far as it *is* exchange value, and does not produce exchange values. It only has exchange value for capital, in so far as it is use value. It is not use value, apart from its exchange value, for the worker himself, but only for capital. Thus the worker exchanges work as a simple exchange value which is predetermined by a past process – he exchanges work itself as objectified labour, only exchanges it in so far as it has already objectified a given amount of labour, so that its equivalent is already measured and given. Capital exchanges it as living labour, as the general productive force of wealth; as activity that increases wealth. Thus it is clear that the worker cannot enrich himself as a result of this exchange, since (like Esau, who exchanged his birthright for a mess of pottage) he gives up his creative power for the ability to work, as an already existing quantity. Rather he is forced to become impoverished, as we shall see later, since the creative power of his work establishes itself against him as an alien force, the power of capital. He alienates himself to work as the productive force of wealth; capital appropriates it as such. The separation of labour and appropriation of the product of labour, the separation of labour and wealth is therefore itself already settled at the time of this act of exchange. What appears to be paradoxical as a result already exists in the very prerequisite. The economists have expressed this more or less empirically. To the worker, therefore, the productivity of his work becomes an alien force. This applies to his work in general, so long as it is genuine work – not assets but activity. Vice versa, capital valorises itself through the appropriation of alien labour. (In this way at least the possibility of valorisation is established, as a result of the exchange between labour and capital. The relationship is first realised in the act of production itself, in which capital actually consumes the alien labour.) Just as, for capital, labour is exchanged as a predetermined exchange value against an equivalent in money, so money is again exchanged against an equivalent in commodities, which are consumed. In this process of exchange, labour is not productive; it becomes productive only for capital; it can only take out of circulation what it has already put in; that is, a predetermined quantity of goods, which is as little its own product as it is its own value. The workers, says Sismondi, exchange their labour for corn, and consume it, whereas the labour 'has become capital for their master' (Sismondi, vi). 'By giving their labour in exchange, the workers transform it into capital' (id. viii). While the worker sells his labour to the capitalists, he retains a right only to the price of labour, not to the product of his labour, nor to the value that labour had added to the product (Cherbuliez, xxviii). 'Selling one's labour = renunciation of all the fruits of labour' (l.c.). All progress in civilisation, therefore, or, in other words, any increase in socially productive forces, in the productive forces of labour itself, if you like – as they come about as a result of science, inventions, the division and combination of labour, improved means of communication, the creation of a world market, machinery, etc. – do not enrich the worker, but only capital; they only serve, therefore, to increase the power that controls labour still further; they merely increase the productive power of capital. Since capital is the opposite of the worker, they only increase objective power over labour. The transformation of labour (as a living purposeful activity) into capital is in itself the result of the exchange between capital and labour, in so far as it gives to the capitalist property rights in the product of labour (and command over labour). This transformation is first of all established in the production process itself. The question whether capital is or is not productive is thus absurd. Labour itself is only productive when taken into capital, when capital forms the basis of production, and the capitalist takes command of production. The productivity of labour likewise becomes the productive force of capital, just as the general exchange value of goods is crystallised in money. Labour, existing for itself in the worker in opposition to capital, i.e. labour in its immediate existence, separated from capital, is not productive. Nor as an activity of the worker will it ever be productive, so long as it only enters into the simple circulation process which only nominally changes its elements. So those who consider that any productive force attributed to capital is a displacement, a transposition, of the productive force of labour, forget that it is capital itself which is essentially this displacement, this transposition. They forget too, that work for wages, as such, presupposes the existence of capital, so that considered from this aspect, it, too, is part of this transubstantiation; this being the necessary process in which its own forces are made alien to the worker. Thus any demand that wage-labour should be allowed to exist and that capital should be abolished is thus self-contradictory and self-invalidating. Other writers – even economists – e.g. Ricardo, Sismondi, etc., state that only labour is productive, not capital. But then they do not leave capital in its specific determined form, as a relationship of production reflected in itself; they think only of a material substance, raw material, etc. These material elements, however, do not make capital into capital. On the other hand it then again occurs to them that capital is, on the one hand, value, in other words it is something immaterial, and indifferent to its material existence. Thus Say wrote: 'Capital always has an immaterial character, since it is not material that produces capital, but the value of this material, a value that has nothing physical about it' (Say, 21). Or Sismondi: 'Capital is a commercial idea' (Sismondi, LX). But then it occurs to them that capital must also be quite another economic category than value, since otherwise there would be nothing to be said about capital as distinguished from value and, if all capital had value, nevertheless this value as such would not yet constitute capital. Then they again seek refuge in its material pattern within the production process, e.g. when Ricardo describes capital as 'accumulated labour employed in the production of new labour', i.e. as a mere instrument of labour or as labour material. In this sense Say even writes about the productive service of capital upon which its remuneration should be based, as though the instrument of labour as such had some pretension to the worker's gratitude, and were not made productive only through him as the instrument of labour. The autonomy of the instrument of labour, i.e. the social definition of it, i.e. its definition as capital, is assumed in such a way that the claims of capital can be deduced. Proudhon's aphorism that 'Capital has value; work produces' means only that capital is value, and here nothing more is said about capital except that it is value, that value is value (the subject of the sentence is here only another name for the predicate), and work produces, or is a productive activity; in other words: labour is labour, because it is nothing but 'producing'. It will be obvious that these tautologies contain no special element of wisdom, and that in particular they cannot express a relationship in which value and work are connected in such a way that they themselves are related and yet are separate from one another, and do not lie alongside one another indifferently. Already the fact that labour occurs in relation to capital as its subject, i.e. that the worker only exists within the definition of work, and that work is not the worker himself, must cause one's eyes to open wide. There is here a connection or relationship, quite apart from capital, of the worker with his own activity which is not in any sense 'natural', but already contains a specifically economic determination.

# 9 Capital as a Productive Force

From *Grundrisse*, pp. 230–2

*Marx describes the historical vocation of capital: to raise the productive forces of society above those necessary for simply reproducing the means of subsistence.*

WHAT appears to be surplus value on the part of capital appears on the worker's side to be, precisely, surplus labour far beyond his requirements, that is to say, far beyond his immediate needs for the maintenance of his livelihood. The great historical feature of capital is that it produces this surplus labour, which is superfluous labour from the standpoint of ordinary use value and mere subsistence. The historical vocation of capital is fulfilled as soon as, on the one hand, demand has developed to the point where there is a general need for surplus labour beyond what is necessary, and surplus labour itself arises from individual needs; and on the other, general industriousness has developed (under the strict discipline of capital) and has been passed on to succeeding generations, until it has become the property of the new generation; and finally when the productive forces of labour, which capital spurs on in its unrestricted desire for wealth and the conditions in which alone capital can achieve this, have developed to the point where the possession and maintenance of general wealth requires, on the one hand, shorter working hours for the whole of society, and working society conducts itself scientifically towards the progressive reproduction of wealth, its reproduction in even greater profusion; so that the sort of labour in which the activities of men can be replaced by those of machines will have ceased. Capital and labour behave in this way like money and goods; if one of them is the general form of wealth, the other is only the substance which aims at immediate consumption. But capital, with its restless striving after the general form of wealth, drives labour out beyond the limits of its natural needs, and thus produces the material elements needed for the development of the rich individuality, which is just as universal in its production as consumption, and whose labour thus itself appears not to be labour any more but a full development of activity, in which the natural necessity has disappeared in its direct form; since the place of natural needs has been taken by needs that are historically produced. This is why capital is productive; it is an essential relationship for the development of the productive forces of society. It only ceases to be so when the development of these productive forces themselves meets a barrier in capital itself.

In *The Times* of November 1857 there appeared a delightful yell of rage from a West Indian planter. With great moral indignation this advocate, in support of his plea for the re-establishment of Negro slavery, described how the Quashees (the free Negroes of Jamaica) were content to produce what was strictly necessary for their own consumption, and looked upon laziness itself ('indulgence and idleness') as the real luxury article alongside this 'use value'. They said that sugar, and all the fixed capital laid out in the plantations, could go to hell; they smirked with ironical, malicious glee at the ruined planters, and even took advantage of the Christianity that they had been taught merely to add a little colour to this gloating resentment and indolence. They had ceased to be slaves, but were not yet wage-earning labourers but only self-sustaining peasants working for their own necessary consumption. Capital, as capital, had no existence in opposition to them, because objectified wealth exists only through either direct forced labour and slavery, or intermediary forced labour, that is, wage-earning labour. Wealth does not stand opposed to direct forced labour as capital, but as a *means* of exercising mastery. Hence, only the means of mastery will be reproduced, for which wealth itself only has value as enjoyment, not as wealth for its own sake, which can therefore never produce industry in general. (We shall return later to this relationship of slavery and wage-earning labour.)

# 10 The Contributions of Labour and Capital to the Production Process

From *Grundrisse*, pp. 264–70

*In this difficult passage, Marx, basing himself on the labour theory of value, analyses the relationship of the contribution of capital and labour to the production process.*

THE increase in values is thus the result of the self-valorisation of capital. It is unimportant whether this self-valorisation is defined as the result of absolute or relative surplus time, i.e. of a real increase of relative surplus labour time, i.e. a decrease of the part of the working day which is the working time required for the maintenance of labour power, necessary labour in general.

Living working time reproduces nothing but the part of the objectified working time (of capital) which appears as the equivalent of the disposition of living labour capacity. This part, as an equivalent, must thus substitute the working time objectified in this labour capacity, i.e. it must substitute the production costs of the active labour power, or in other words it must maintain the existence of the worker as a worker. What is further produced by this working time is not a reproduction but a new creation, and indeed a new creation of values, since there is objectification of new working time in use value. The fact that the working time contained in the raw material and in the instrument is maintained simultaneously is the result not of the amount of labour but of its quality as labour in general, its general quality, which is not linked to any particular one of its aspects and is not specifically defined labour. Labour, considered as labour, is labour, and is not specially paid for as such, since capital has bought this quality from the worker by means of exchange.

But the measured equivalent of this quality (the specific use value of labour) is simply the *quantity* of working time that it has produced. The worker begins by adding so many new forms to the value of the raw material and the instrument, through the utilisa tion of the instrument as an instrument and the transformation of raw material, as would equal the working time that is contained in his own wages. Anything more that he adds is surplus working time, surplus value. But through the simple relationship that the instrument is used as an instrument, and the raw material is treated as the raw material of labour; through the simple process involved in their coming into contact with labour and being constituted as its means and object and thus as an objectification of active labour, and factors of labour itself, they are conserved not in their form but in their substance. Economically considered, objectified working time is their substance. Objectified working time ceases to exist in a one-sided objectified form, and hence ceases to be the victim, as a mere object, of the (as it were) chemical process of dissolution, since it is constituted as the material means of existence (the means and the object) of living labour. From the purely objectified labour time, in whose real existence labour only exists as a vanished, external form of its natural substance, which is itself external to the substance (e.g. wood in the shape of a table, or iron in the shape of a roller), merely having an existence in the outer, material form, there develops the indifference of the substance to the form. Labour does not retain the form through any living inherent law of reproduction, as the tree, for example, keeps its form as a tree (the wood is retained as a tree in a particular form, since this form is one of the forms of wood; whereas the form as a table is accidental to the wood, not the inherent shape of its substance). Labour thus exists only as the form external to the material, or it exists itself only materially. The disintegration to which its material is exposed also involves its own disintegration. But when matter is regarded as the conditioning factor of living labour, then it again becomes animated. Objectified labour ceases to exist as a dead, external, indifferent form, since it again constitutes a factor of living labour, a connection of living labour to itself in objective material, as the *objectivity* of living labour (as means and object) (the *objective* conditions of living labour). Thus living labour itself through its realisation in the material changes this material; this change is determined by the purpose of the labour and its purposeful activity (a change that is not, as in the dead object, the imposition of the form as outside the substance, merely the vanishing appearance of its existence); and the material is thus maintained in a particular form, the change in form of the substance being subjected to the purpose of the labour. Labour is the living fire that shapes the pattern; it is the transitoriness of things, their temporality, their transformation by living time. In the simple production process – apart from the process of valorisation – the transitoriness of the form of things is used in order to establish their utility. When yarn is made from cotton, and textiles from the yarn, and printed patterns on coloured fabric from textiles, and out of these, say a garment:

1. The substance of the cotton has been retained in all these forms. (In the chemical process, (natural) equivalents have been exchanged in the metabolism of material that has been regulated by labour.)

2. In all these subsequent processes, the material has gained a more useful form, as being more appropriate to consumption; until it has finally reached the form in which it can be the direct object of consumption, in which, thus, the consumption of the material and its conversion to the benefit of mankind take place, so that the change is itself its use. The cotton material is retained throughout all these processes; it is lost in one form of use value, *in order to make way for a higher form, until the object exists as an object of immediate consumption.* But since the cotton is wound in the form of twist, it is placed in a definite relationship to a different type of work. Should this work not take place, not only is the form which it has been given useless, i.e. the earlier work will not be endorsed by the later work, but the material itself is spoilt, in that in the form of twist it only has use value so long as it is once more processed; it only has use value in so far as it is related to the use that further work will make of it; it only has use value in so far as its form as twist is turned into that of fabric; while the cotton, in its existence as cotton, is capable of being used in endless ways. Thus, without further work, the use value of cotton and twist, both matter and form, would be spoilt; it would be destroyed rather than produced. The material, like the form, the cloth, like the form, will be retained as use value by further work, until it has

reached the shape of use value as such, whose use is consumption. Thus it is implicit in the simple production process that the early stage of production is maintained by the later stage, and that through the establishment of the higher use value the older value will be kept up, or only altered in so far as it is raised as use value. It is living labour that retains the use value of the unfinished labour product, in making it the material for further labour. But it only retains it, i.e. only protects it from uselessness and disappearance, in that it manufactures it to suit its purpose, makes it generally the object of new living labour. This *retention of the old use value* is not a process that occurs apart from the increase or completion of this value through fresh labour; rather, it is produced through the increase of use value itself by fresh labour. In the same way that weaving labour transforms yarn into fabric, i.e. treats it as the raw material of weaving (and the twist only has use value once it has been woven) – and weaving is a special kind of living labour – it retains the use value that belonged to the cotton as such, and is specifically retained in the yarn. It keeps the product of labour, in that it makes it into the raw material of fresh labour; but (1) it does not add any fresh labour, and (2) it keeps the use value of the raw material through other labour. It keeps the usefulness of cotton as yarn in weaving the yarn. (All this belongs to the first chapter of 'Production in general'.) It keeps it through the weaving. This retention of the labour as product, or of the use value of the product of labour, so that it can be made into the raw material of fresh labour, and is again established as the material objectivity of purposeful living labour, is inherent in the simple production process. In relation to use value, labour possesses the property of retaining it by increasing it, and it increases it by making it the object of fresh labour determined by its final purpose; remakes it from the form of indifferent existence into that of objective material, the body of labour. (This also applies to the instrument. A spindle only retains its use value so long as it is used for spinning. Otherwise both the labour that set up the definite form (made in this case of iron and wood) and the material out of which the definite form was made, would both be spoilt for use. Only if it is established as a means of living work, as an objective element in the existence of its animation, will the use value of wood and iron as well as its form be retained.

Its purpose as an instrument implies that it is to be used, but used in the spinning process. The greater productivity that it imparts to work creates more use value, and thus replaces the use value that has been used up in the consumption of the instrument. This appears most clearly in agriculture, because the instrument appears in its simplest and original form directly as foodstuff and use value, as distinguished from exchange value. When the farmer's hoe obtains for him twice as much corn as he could otherwise obtain, he needs to devote less time to the production of the hoe itself; he has provision enough to make himself a new hoe). Now the components of capital that constitute its value – one of them existing in the form of material and the other in the form of the instrument – make their appearance in the process of valorisation as opposed to the worker, that is, to living labour (since the worker exists as such only in this process), not as values, but as simple factors in the production process; as use value for labour, as the objective conditions of its effectiveness, or as its objective elements. The fact that the worker conserves these use values while he is using the instrument as an instrument and is giving a higher form of use value to the raw material, lies in the nature of labour itself. But the use values of labour retained in this way are exchange values when considered as components of capital, and determined as such through the production costs retained in them, the quantity of objectified work contained in them. (For use value is only concerned with the quality of the already objectified work.) The quantity of objectified labour will be retained in that its quality as use value for further labour will remain through contact with living labour. The use value of the cotton, like its use value as yarn, will be retained to the extent that it is woven as yarn, to the extent that it exists as one of the objective elements (with the spinning-wheel) in weaving. In this way there is also retained the quantity of working time that was contained in the cotton and the cotton yarn. What appears in the simple production process to be the retention of the quality of the previous work – and thus also of the material in which it is established – appears in the process of valorisation as the retention of the quantity of the already objectified labour. For capital, this is a retention of the quantity of objectified labour through the production process; for living labour it is only the retention of the use value which is already present, and present for labour. Living labour adds a new quantity of work; but it does not retain the already objectified quantity of work through this quantitative addition; it does this through its quality as living labour, in that it relates itself as labour to the use values in which previous labour exists. But living labour is not paid for this quality that it possesses as living labour – it would not be bought at all if it were not living labour – only for the quantity of work that is actually contained in it. Only the price of its use value is paid for, as with that of all other goods. The specific quality that it possesses, in that it adds a fresh quantity of labour to the quantity of already objectified labour and at the same time retains objectified labour in its quality as objectified labour, is not paid to it, and also costs the worker nothing, since this is the natural property of his labour power. In the production process, the separation of labour from its objectified elements of existence – instrument and material – is abolished. The existence of capital and wage-labour depends on this separation. The abolition of the separation, which really takes place in the production process – for otherwise there could be no work at all – is not paid for by capital. (The abolition also occurs not through the exchange with the worker, but through the work itself in the production process. But, as such actual work, it is itself already incorporated in capital; it is an element of capital. This retaining power of labour thus appears as the self-retention force of capital. The worker has only added fresh work; the past work – while capital exists – has an eternal existence as value, completely independent of its material being. This is how things look both to the worker and to capital.) If capital had to pay for this abolition it would cease to be capital. This abolition is contained within the material role that labour plays, according to its nature, in the production process contained in its use value. But as use value, labour belongs to the capitalist; it only belongs to the worker as a mere exchange value. Its living quality in the production process itself, enabling it to retain objectified working time in such a way that it makes it into the objective existence of living labour, is no concern of the worker. This process of appropriation, whereby in the production process itself living labour makes the instrument and the material into the body of its soul, and thus raises them from the dead, is, in fact, in contrast to the fact that labour is deprived of its objects, or only real in terms of direct animation of the worker – and labour material as well as instrument have an existence of their own within capital. (Return to this later.) The valorisation process of capital occurs through and in the simple production process, in that living labour is placed in its natural relationship to its material elements of existence. But to the extent that it enters into this relationship, the relationship exists not for labour itself, but for capital; it is itself already an element of capital.

# 11 Capital as a Revolutionary, but Limited, Force

From *Grundrisse*, pp. 313–14

*In this passage Marx pursues the well-known theme of the opening passages of the* Communist Manifesto *on capital as a revolutionary and civilising force. He goes on to point out that capital has limitations which, in order to be overcome, will lead to its own abolition.*

THUS on the one hand production which is founded on capital creates universal industry – i.e. surplus labour, value-producing labour; on the other hand it creates a system of general exploitation of natural human attributes, a system of general profitability, whose vehicles seem to be just as much science, as all the physical and intellectual characteristics. There is nothing which can escape, by its own elevated nature or self-justifying characteristics, from this cycle of social production and exchange. Thus capital first creates bourgeois society and the universal appropriation of nature and of social relationships themselves by the members of society. Hence the great civilising influence of capital, its production of a stage of society compared with which all earlier stages appear to be merely *local progress* and idolatry of nature. Nature becomes for the first time simply an object for mankind, purely a matter of utility; it ceases to be recognised as a power in its own right; and the theoretical knowledge of its independent laws appears only as a stratagem designed to subdue it to human requirements, whether as the object of consumption or as the means of production. Pursuing this tendency, capital has pushed beyond national boundaries and prejudices, beyond the deification of nature and the inherited, self-sufficient satisfaction of existing needs confined within well-defined bounds, and the reproduction of the traditional way of life. It is destructive of all this, and permanently revolutionary, tearing down all obstacles that impede the development of productive forces, the expansion of needs, the diversity of production and the exploitation and exchange of natural and intellectual forces.

But because capital sets up any such boundary as a limitation, and is thus *ideally* over and beyond it, it does not in any way follow that it has *really* surmounted it, and since any such limitation contradicts its vocation, capitalist production moves in contradictions which are constantly overcome, only to be, again, constantly re-established. Still more so. The universality towards which it is perpetually driving finds limitations in its own nature, which at a certain stage of its development will make it appear as itself the greatest barrier to this tendency, leading thus to its own self-destruction.

# 12 Alienated Labour and Capital

From *Grundrisse*, pp. 354–9

*Marx returns, in this passage, to themes of the* Paris Manuscripts *and places his account of alienated labour in the context of his ideas on surplus labour and surplus value. He is
concerned to show in particular how labour creates its own
alienation.*

THE additional value is thus again established as capital, as
objectified labour entering into the exchange process with living
labour, and thence dividing itself into a constant part – the
objective conditions of labour, the existence of living labour power,
the necessaries, food for the worker. In this second appearance of
capital in this form, some points are cleared up which in its first
appearance – as money, which is changing from the form of value
into that of capital – were completely obscure. They are now
solved through the process of valorisation and production. At
their first occurrence, the prerequisites themselves seemed to be
exterior and derived from circulation; thus they did not arise
from its internal nature, nor were they explained by it. These
external prerequisites will now appear as elements in the movement of capital itself, so that capital itself has presupposed them
as its own elements, irrespective of how they arose historically.

Within the production process itself, surplus value – the surplus
value solicited as a result of the constraint of capital – appeared
as surplus labour and even as living labour, which, however, since
it cannot produce anything from nothing, finds its own objective
conditions in advance. Now this surplus labour appears objectified
as surplus product, and this surplus product, in order to valorise
itself as capital, divides itself into a double form: as objective
labour conditions (material and instrument) and as subjective
labour conditions (food) for the living labour now to be put to

work. The general form of value – objectified labour – and objectified labour arising from circulation is, naturally, the general and self-evident presupposition. Further: the surplus product in its totality – which objectifies surplus labour in its totality – now appears as surplus capital (as compared with the original capital, before it had undertaken this circulation), i.e. as autonomous exchange value, which is opposed to the living labour power as its specific use value. All the factors which were opposed to the living labour power as forces which were alien, external, and which consumed and utilised the living labour power under definite conditions which were themselves independent of it, are now established as its own product and result.

1. The surplus value or surplus product is nothing but a definite amount of objectified living labour – the sum of the surplus labour. This new value, which is opposed to living labour as an independent value to be exchanged against it, in fact as capital, is the product of labour. It is itself nothing but the general superfluity of labour over necessary labour – in an objective form, and thus as a value.

2. The special shapes that are assumed by this value in order to revalorise itself, i.e. to establish itself as capital – on the one hand as raw material and instrument, on the other as means of subsistence for labour during the act of production – are likewise, therefore, only special forms of surplus labour itself. Raw material and instrument are produced from it in such circumstances – or it itself becomes objective as raw material and instrument in such a proportion – that a definite sum of necessary work (necessary in the sense that it is living, and produces the means of subsistence which are its value) can be objectified in the surplus labour, and indeed incessantly objectified, in other words it can again continue the division of the objective and subjective conditions of its self-maintenance and self-reproduction. Moreover, while living labour is executing the process that reproduces its objective conditions, it has at the same time established raw material and instrument in such proportions that – as surplus labour, as labour beyond what is necessary – it can realise itself in them, and thus make them into material to create new values. The objective conditions of surplus labour – which are limited to the proportion of raw material and instrument above the requirements of necessary

labour, while the objective conditions of necessary labour are divided within their objectivity into objective and subjective, into material elements of labour and subjective elements (means of subsistence for living labour) – thus now appear and are thus established as the product, the result, the objective form, the external existence of surplus labour itself. Originally, on the other hand, this seemed alien to living labour itself, as though capital was responsible for the fact that instrument and means of subsistence were present to such an extent that it was possible for living labour to realise itself not only as necessary labour but as surplus labour.

3. The independent and autonomous existence of value as against living labour power –

hence its existence as capital –

the objective, self-centred indifference, the alien nature of objective conditions of labour as against living labour power, reaching the point that –

(1) these conditions face the worker, as a person, in the person of the capitalist (as personifications with their own will and interest), this absolute separation and divorce of ownership (i.e. of the material conditions of labour from living labour power); these conditions are opposed to the worker as alien property, as the reality of another legal person and the absolute domain of their will –

and that

(2) labour hence appears as alien labour as opposed to the value personified in the capitalist or to the conditions of labour –

this absolute divorce between property and labour, between living labour power and the conditions of its realisation, between objectified and living labour, between the value and the activity that creates value –

hence also the alien nature of the content of the work vis-à-vis the worker himself –

this separation now also appears as the product of labour itself, as an objectification of its own elements.

For through the new act of production itself (which merely confirmed the exchange between capital and living labour that had preceded it), surplus labour and thus surplus value, surplus product, in brief, the total result of labour (that of surplus labour as well as of necessary labour) is established as capital, as exchange value which is independently and indifferently opposed both to living labour power and to its mere use value.

Labour power has only adopted the subjective conditions of necessary labour – subsistence indispensable for productive labour power, i.e. its reproduction merely as labour power divorced from the conditions of its realisation – and it has itself set up these conditions as objects and values, which stand opposed to it in an alien and authoritarian personification.

It comes out of this process not only no richer but actually poorer than when it entered it. For not only do the conditions of necessary labour that it has produced belong to capital; but also the possibility of creating values which is potentially present in labour power now likewise exists as surplus value, surplus product, in a word, as capital, as dominion over living labour power, as value endowed with its own strength and will as opposed to the abstract, purposeless, purely subjective poverty of labour power. Labour power has not only produced alien wealth and its own poverty, but also the relationship of this intrinsic wealth to itself as poverty, through the consumption of which wealth puts new life into itself and again makes itself fruitful. This all arose from the exchange in which labour power exchanged its living power for a quantity of objectified labour, except that this objectified labour, – these conditions of its existence which exist outside it, and the independent external nature of these material conditions – appears as its own product. These conditions appear as though set up by labour power itself, both as its own objectification, and as the objectification of its own power which has an existence independent of it and, even more, rules over it, rules over it by its own doing.

In surplus capital all the elements are the product of alien labour – the alien surplus labour which has been changed into capital: means of subsistence for the necessary work; the objective conditions (material and instrument), so that the necessary labour can reproduce the value exchanged against it as means of subsistence; finally, the necessary quantity of materials and instruments with which new surplus labour can be realised within it or new surplus value produced.

Here we see the disappearance of the semblance that existed when the production process was first considered, to the effect that capital brought some value with it out of the circulation. The objective conditions of labour now appear to be much more its own product – so far, that is, as they have value in general or use value for production. But if capital thus appears as the product of labour, the product of labour also appears as capital – no more as a simple product, nor as exchangeable goods, but as capital; objectified labour assumes mastery, has command over living labour. It appears just as much the product of labour that its product appears as alien property, an independent mode of existence opposed to living labour, and equally autonomous value; that the product of labour, objectified labour, has acquired its own soul from living labour and has established itself opposite living labour as an alien force. Considered from the standpoint of labour, labour thus appears to be active in the production process in such a way that it seems to reject its realisation in objective conditions as alien reality, and that it puts itself in the position of an insubstantial labour power endowed only with needs against this reality which is estranged from it and which belongs, not to it, but to others. Labour appears to establish its own reality, not as an entity of its own, but merely as an entity for others, and thus also as a mere entity of others, or other entity, against itself. This process of realisation is similarly the de-realisation process of labour. It establishes itself objectively, but it establishes this objectivity as its own non-being or as the being of its non-being – of capital. It returns to itself as a mere potentiality of creating values or valorisation; since the entire real wealth, the world of real value and likewise the real conditions of its own realisation are placed in opposition to it as entities with an independent existence. These are the possibilities that are resting in the womb of living labour, but which exist as realities outside it as a result of the production process – but as realities that are alien to it, that build up wealth in opposition to it.

In so far as the surplus product is valorised afresh as surplus capital, and re-enters the production process and the self-valorisation process, it is divided into (1) means of subsistence for the workers, to be exchanged against living labour power; this part of capital can be described as the labour fund. This labour fund –

the part designed for the maintenance of the labour power, and
for its progressive maintenance, since surplus capital constantly
grows – now appears just as much as the product of alien labour,
labour alien to capital, as (2) its other components – the material
conditions for the reproduction of a value = these means of subsistence + a surplus value.

Further, when this surplus capital is considered, capital is
divided into two parts, one constant, the other variable: the constant part – raw material and instruments of labour – was antediluvian and existed earlier than labour itself; the variable part
consisted of the means of subsistence that could be exchanged
against living labour power. However, this division appears to be
purely formal, for both parts are at the same time produced by
labour, and yet function as the prerequisites of labour. This division of capital within itself appears more as though labour's own
product – objectified surplus labour – is divided into two components: (1) the objective conditions for fresh valorisation of
labour, and (2) a fund of labour for maintaining the possibility
of this living labour, i.e. this living labour power considered as
living labour but in such a way that the labour power can only
again appropriate that part of its own result which has been
defined as a labour fund (the result of its own being in objective
form), can only bring it out of the form of the alien wealth that
opposes it on condition that it not only reproduces its value, but
also valorises the part of the fresh capital which represents the
objective conditions for the realisation of new surplus labour and
surplus production, or production of surplus values. Labour itself
has created a new fund for the use of new necessary labour, or,
which amounts to the same thing, a fund for the maintenance of
new living labour power – workers – but at the same time the
condition that this fund can only be utilised so long as new surplus
labour is applied to the superfluous part of surplus capital. In the
surplus capital produced by labour – surplus value – the real need
for new surplus labour is created at the same time, and thus
surplus capital itself represents the real feasibility of both new
surplus labour and new surplus capital. This makes it clear how
the objective world of wealth progressively extends through labour
itself as a force alien to it, and achieves an ever wider and fuller
existence, so that relatively, in relation to the values created or

the real conditions of the creation of value, the indigent subjective world of living labour power forms an ever more glaring contrast. The more labour objectifies itself, the greater will be the objective world of values that faces it in the form of alien property. Through the creation of surplus capital, labour lays on itself the necessity of creating new surplus capital once more, etc., etc.

In relation to the original non-surplus capital, the circumstances have changed so far as labour power is concerned, in that (1) the part of it that is exchanged against necessary labour is reproduced by this labour itself, i.e. it no longer comes from the circulation, but is its own product; and (2) the part of the value which represents, in the raw material and instrument, the conditions for the valorisation of living labour, is retained by living labour itself in the production process, and since each use value exists according to its nature in transitory material, whereas the exchange value is only there – only exists – in use value, this retention = a protection against the downfall or negation of the transitory nature of the values possessed by the capitalists; hence its establishment as value existing for itself, as non-transitory wealth. This original sum-total of values is thus first of all established as capital in the production process by living labour.

# 13 Property as the Right to Alien Labour

From *Grundrisse*, pp. 360–2

*Marx here attempts to explain how property was originally defined in terms of man's products; but that with the growth of capitalism products no longer belong to the worker but to the capitalist, who does not even acquire them by exchange since what he exchanges for them is previously appropriated surplus labour.*

Now, from the standpoint of capital: as far as surplus capital is concerned, the capitalist represents value as an entity in itself, the third function of money – wealth, through the mere acquisition of alien labour, in that each element of surplus capital – material, instrument and means of subsistence – is resolved into alien labour, which the capitalist does not acquire by means of exchange for existing values, but which he has acquired without exchange. Of course the original condition for this surplus capital was the exchange of a part of the values belonging to the capitalist, or the objectified labour that he possesses, against alien living labour power. Let us term surplus capital, as it originated from the first production process, surplus capital I. For the creation of this capital, i.e. for the acquisition of alien labour, of objectified alien labour, a condition appears to be the possession of values on the part of the capitalist, of which he exchanges one part, as a matter of form, for living labour capacity. We say 'as a matter of form' because living labour has to replace and give back again the exchanged values. But he can please himself about this. In any case the condition for the existence of surplus capital I, i.e. for the acquisition of alien labour or of the values in which it has been objectified, appears as the exchange of the values belonging to the capitalist, placed by him into the circulation, and conveyed by him to living labour power – but which do not derive capital from

its exchange with living labour, nor from the relationship of
capital to labour.

Let us now think of surplus capital as having been again thrown
into the production process, so that it again realises its surplus
value in exchange, and once more appears as new surplus capital
at the beginning of a third process of production. This surplus
capital II has different prerequisites from surplus capital I. The
prerequisites of surplus capital I were the values that belonged to
the capitalist and were placed by him in the circulation, or more
precisely, to be exchanged for living labour power. The prerequisite of surplus capital II is nothing more than the existence of
surplus capital I; in other words, the prerequisite that the capitalist has already appropriated alien labour without any exchange.
This puts him in the position of being able to begin the process
all over again. Of course, in order to create surplus capital II, one
part of the value of surplus capital I must be exchanged for living
labour power in the form of means of subsistence; but what he
thus exchanged consisted of original values, which he did not
bring into circulation from his own funds; they consisted, on the
contrary, of alien objectified labour, which he had acquired without offering any equivalent and which he now again exchanges for
alien living labour, and also of the material, etc., in which this
new labour becomes realised and in which it creates surplus value,
which has come into his hands without any exchange but merely
as a result of his having appropriated it. The past appropriation
of alien labour is thus the simple condition for fresh appropriation
of alien labour; or alien labour is found to be the property of the
capitalist objectively (materially) in the form cf existing values,
and this is the condition that enables him to appropriate anew
the alien living labour power, and thence surplus labour, which is
labour without any equivalent. The fact that the capitalist was
already in opposition to living labour is the only condition not
only for his self-retention as capital, but also for his appropriation,
as growing capital, of more and more alien labour without equivalent; and as regards labour power, these rights change into the
duty to behave towards its own work or its own product as to alien
property. Proprietary rights change dialectically on the one hand
into the right to appropriate alien labour, and on the other into
the duty to respect the product of its own labour, and its own

labour itself, as values belonging to others. The exchange of equivalents, however, which appeared to be the original operation which legally expressed the proprietorial rights, has become so twisted that on the one hand there is only the semblance of an exchange, since the part of capital which was exchanged for living labour power is in the first place itself alien labour, acquired without equivalent, and in the second place must be replaced by a surplus of labour power; in fact it is not really ceded, but only changed from one form into another. The exchange relationship has thus completely vanished, or remains only as an illusion. It also seemed originally that proprietary rights were founded on the worker's own labour. But now property appears as the right to appropriate alien labour, and the impossibility of labour appropriating its own product for itself. The complete divorce between property (still more, wealth) and labour thus appears as the consequence of the law that originally identified them.

Finally the production and valorisation process seems to result in the reproduction and fresh production of the relationship between capital and labour itself, the relationship between capitalist and worker. This social relationship, or production relationship, appears in fact to be a still more important result of the process than its material results. The worker, in fact, produces himself within the process, as labour power and as the capital that opposes him, just as, on the other side, the capitalist produces himself as capital, as well as the living labour power that opposes him. Each one reproduces himself in that at the same time he produces his opposite, his negation. The capitalist produces labour as something alien to itself; and labour produces its product, also as something alien. The capitalist produces the worker and the worker produces the capitalist, etc. . . .

# 14 Exchange Relationships in Feudal and Capitalist Society

From *Grundrisse*, pp. 363–74

*Marx here analyses the difference between exchange in medieval society and exchange in capitalist society. In the former there is an exchange of services or objects which only have a use value. In the latter, value as such, permitting the creation of surplus value, dominates exchange. There are digressions on the alienation of labour in capitalist society, and, at the end of the section, a discussion of the impact of machinery on this alienation.*

MONEY has in fact only been turned into capital at the end of the first production process which results in its reproduction and the new production of surplus capital I. But surplus capital I is itself only established as surplus capital, and realised as such, once it has produced surplus capital II; once, in fact, the prerequisites of the transition of money into capital, which are still external to the movement of real capital, have disappeared, and capital has in fact established the conditions, in line with its inherent nature, for entering production. Once we assume this production is founded on capital, the condition that the capitalist must introduce into circulation values that he has created – whether through his own labour or otherwise, since he does not yet have available wage-labour, either present or past – in order to set himself up as a capitalist, now belongs to the antediluvian conditions of capital; it belongs to its historical prerequisites, which already as such are past, and thus belong to the history of its development and not in any way to its contemporary history, i.e. not to the real system of the mode of production that it controls. If, for example, the flight of the serfs to the towns was one of the historical conditions and prerequisites of the urban system, it ceases to be a condition, and a factor in its reality, once the towns have developed. It belongs, on the contrary, to their past prerequisites, to the prerequisites of their development, that are done away with once they are established. The conditions and prerequisites of the development, of the coming into being, of capital thus in fact imply that it does not yet exist, but that it will; thus they disappear as capital becomes reality, as capital itself, proceeding from its reality, establishes the conditions for its realisation. Thus in the original transition from money, or value existing in its own right, to capital, there is presupposed an accumulation by the capitalist (achieved, perhaps, by saving the products or values created by his own labour), which he accomplished before he was a capitalist. Thus although money becomes capital as a result of prerequisites which are determined and external to capital, as soon as capital as such has come into existence, it creates its own prerequisites, namely the possession of real conditions for the creation of new values without exchange – through its own process of production. These prerequisites, which were originally conditions of its formation – and thus could not yet arise from its action as capital – now appear as the results of its own realisation, its own reality, as established by it – not as the condition of its coming into being, but as the result of its existence. Capital no longer proceeds from prerequisites in order to develop; it is its own prerequisite, and proceeds from itself, creating the presuppositions of its maintenance and growth. Thus the conditions that preceded the creation of surplus capital i, or expressed the formation of capital, do not come within the sphere of means of production, of which capital is a prerequisite. They are historical stages of its development, just as the processes whereby the earth changed from a fluid sea of fire and steam into its present form now lie beyond its existence as a completed world. This means that individual capital can still be formed, for example by hoarding. The hoard is, however, only changed into capital by exploitation of labour. Bourgeois economists, who consider capital to be an eternal, natural (and not historical) form of production, are always seeking to justify it, in that they portray the conditions of its formation as the conditions of its present realisation. They present the conditions in which the capitalist (because he is still developing into a capitalist) still has a non-capitalist mode of appropriation as the very conditions of capitalist appropriation.

These attempts at apology indicate a bad conscience, and an inability to harmonise the means of appropriation of capital, as capital, with the general laws of property proclaimed by capitalist society itself. On the other hand, and this is much more important for us, our method shows the points where the historical approach must be introduced, and where the bourgeois economy, as a purely historical aspect of the production process, is related to historically earlier means of production. Therefore it is not necessary, in order to analyse the laws of the bourgeois economy, to write the true history of production relationships. But the correct approach to them and deduction of them as historically developed relationships always lead us to draw comparisons based on the past history of this system as, for example, with the empirical figures of natural science. These illusions, together with a correct grasp of the present day, thus also offer a key to the understanding of the past. This is a task in itself, which we hope to reach in due course. Equally, this correct interpretation leads us to points that suggest the abolition of the present mode of production and foreshadow the future. Thus while the pre-bourgeois phases appear to be only historical, i.e. terminated, prerequisites, so the present conditions of production can be seen as self-terminating, and thus at the same time as establishing historical presuppositions for a new kind of society.

Let us next consider the realised relationship, value realised as capital and living labour as mere use value opposed to capital, so that living labour seems to be merely a means whereby the objectified, dead labour can be valorised, given a living soul, and loses its own thereby. This results in wealth that has been created as something alien; only the growing impoverishment of living labour power is its own. Here the position is thus simply that in and through the process itself the real material conditions of living labour – material in which it can be valorised; instrument with which it can valorise itself; and means of subsistence with which the flame of living labour can be fanned and protected from becoming extinguished, and the necessary fuel added for its continued life – these conditions are fixed as an alien, independent existence, or as the means of existence of an alien person, as autonomous and opposed to living labour power, which also exists subjectively in isolation from them, as self-sufficient, autonomous values which develop wealth that is alien to labour power, the wealth of the capitalist. The objective conditions of living labour appear as separate, objectified values, opposed to living labour power, which, as a subjective existence, is opposed to them only as the value of another kind (differing from them not as value, but as use value). Once this separation has been established, the production process can only produce it again, reproduce it, and reproduce it on a greater scale. We have seen how it does this. The objective conditions of living labour power are presupposed as existing independently from it, as the objectivity of a subject which is different from living labour power and independently opposed to it. Reproduction and valorisation, i.e. the extension of these objective conditions, are thus at the same time the reproduction and fresh production of them as the wealth of an alien subject, indifferently and independently opposed to labour power. The thing that is reproduced and newly produced is not only the existence of these objective conditions of living labour, but their existence in the form of independent values belonging to others, and opposed to this living labour power. The objective conditions of labour retain a subjective existence opposed to living labour power, since out of capital there develops the capitalist. On the other hand the purely subjective existence of labour power as opposed to its own conditions gives it a quite indifferent objective form as opposed to them. It is only a value with special use value, alongside the conditions of its own valorisation as values of another use value. These values do not become realised in the production process as conditions of the realisation of labour power; on the contrary, labour power emerges from the production process as the simple condition of their valorisation as independent values opposed to it. The raw material that it works on is alien material; likewise the instrument is an alien instrument; its labour occurs only as an accessory to their substance, and thus objectifies itself in what does not belong to it. Even living labour itself appears to be alien as opposed to living labour power, whose labour it is, whose own manifestation of life it is, since it has been ceded to capital in exchange for objectified labour, produced by labour itself. Labour power behaves towards labour as though to something alien, and if capital felt inclined to pay the worker without obliging him to work, the latter would readily accept the offer. His own labour (and also its orientation) is thus just as alien as are the material and the instrument. Thus the product appears to him as an alien combination of material, instrument and labour, as alien property; when production is finished, labour is impoverished because of the vital force that it has expended, and yet the drudgery has to begin again, the purely subjective labour power being divorced from its means of existence. When the worker recognises the products as being his own and condemns the separation of the conditions of his realisation as an intolerable imposition, it will be an enormous progress in consciousness, itself the product of the method of production based on capital, and a death-knell of capital in the same way that once the slaves became aware that they were persons, that they did not need to be the property of others, the continued existence of slavery could only vegetate on as an artificial thing, and could not continue to be the basis of production.

Let us, on the other hand, consider the original relationship which existed before money entered into the self-valorisation process. Various conditions have to originate historically or be present before money becomes capital and labour becomes wage-labour which establishes and creates capital. ('Wage-labour' is here used in the strict economic sense in which alone we need it – we shall later have to distinguish it from other forms of labour for a daily wage, etc. – as labour that establishes and produces capital, i.e. living labour, which at the same time produces both the objective conditions for its realisation as an activity, and the objective elements of its existence as labour power, as alien forces opposing it, as values which are independent of it and exist for themselves alone.) The essential conditions are established in the relationship as it originally exists:

1. On the one hand, living labour power is present as a purely subjective existence, separated from the elements of its objective reality; thus it is separated just as much from the conditions of living labour as from the means of subsistence and self-preservation of living labour power; in fact, there is on the one hand the active possibility of labour in all its abstraction.

2. On the other hand there is value, or objectified labour. This must be an accumulation of use values large enough to provide the objective conditions, not merely for the production of products or

values needed in order to reproduce or maintain living labour power, but also to absorb surplus labour. In short, there must be objective material for labour.

3. There must be a free exchange relationship (money circulation) between the two sides, founded on exchange values, not on the master–servant relationship. There must be a mediation between the two extremes. This means production which does not deliver the means of subsistence directly to the producer, but arranges it through exchange, and since it cannot gain control of the alien labour directly, buys it by means of exchange from the worker.

4. Finally the side representing the objective conditions of labour in the form of independent, self-sufficient values must take the form of value and have as its ultimate purpose the setting up of values, self-valorisation and the creation of money – and not the immediate enjoyment or the creation of use value.

So long as both sides can only exchange their labour with one another in the form of objectified labour, this relationship is impossible; it is equally impossible when living labour power itself is the property of the other side and not something to be exchanged. (This does not entirely rule out the possibility of the existence of slavery at isolated points within the bourgeois production system. But this is only possible because it does not exist at other points of the system and appears as an anomaly in opposition to the bourgeois system itself.)

The conditions in which this relationship originally appears or which appear to be historical presuppositions of its formation, seem at first sight to have a double-sided nature – the dissolution of primitive forms of living labour on the one hand, and the dissolution of its happier relationships on the other.

The first prerequisite is that the system of slavery or bondage should be abolished. Living labour power belongs to itself, and disposes of its own manifestation of force by means of exchange. Both sides are opposed to one another as persons. Formally, their relationship is the free and equal one of those who exchange. It appears that this is a mere semblance, and a deceptive semblance, as soon as we consider the legal relationship outside the sphere of strict economics. What the free worker sells is always only a definite, particular quantity of manifestation of force; and labour power as a totality dominates each particular manifestation. The worker sells his particular power to a particular capitalist, facing him independently as an individual. But it is clear that this is not his relationship to the existence of capital as capital, i.e. to the capitalist class. Nevertheless, as far as he is concerned as a real, individual person, he sees opening before him a vast field of arbitrary choice, and thus formal freedom. In the slavery relationship the worker belongs to an individual, particular owner, whose labour machine he is. In all the force that he can manifest, all his labour power, he belongs to another, and thus is not related as a subject to his own particular manifestation of force or his living act of working. In the bondage relationship, the worker is an element of landed property; he is a chattel of the earth just as cattle are. In the slave relationship the worker is nothing but a living machine, who as a result has a value for others, or rather is a value for others. Labour power seems to the free worker to be entirely his property, one of his elements which he, as a subject, controls, and which he retains in selling it. We shall develop this further in the section on wage-labour.

The exchange of objectified labour against living labour does not suffice to constitute one side as being capital, the other as wage-labour. The whole class of the so-called providers of services, from the shoeshine boy to the king, falls into this category. So also does the free wage-earner, whom we find everywhere to a sporadic extent, in places where either the oriental or the occidental community (consisting of free landed proprietors) dissolves into its individual elements – as a result of increase in population, release of prisoners of war, accidental conditions in which there is impoverishment of the individual and the objective circumstances of his self-sustaining labour disappear, as a result of the division of labour, etc. When A exchanges either value or money, i.e. objectified labour, in order to obtain a service from B, that is, living labour, this can occur:

1. In the relationship of simple circulation. Both, in fact, only exchange use values: one of them, means of subsistence; the other exchanges his labour, which is a service that the first desires to consume either directly (personal service), or by supplying the material by means of which, through his labour, through the objectification of his labour, the second creates use value destined

to be consumed by the first. As, for example, when a farmer admits a travelling tailor into his house (as used to happen in the past) and gives him the cloth to make clothes with. Or if I give a doctor money to patch up my health for me. What is important in such cases is the service that they render to each other. *Do ut facias*[1] seems here to be on exactly the same level as *facio ut des*[2] or *do ut des*.[3] The man who makes me a suit out of the cloth for which I have supplied him the material, gives me a use value. But instead of giving it at once in the objectified form, he gives it in the form of an activity. I give him a ready-made use value; he transforms it into another one for me. The difference between past, objectified and living, present labour appears here only as the formal difference between the various *tenses* of the work, which at one time occur in the perfect tense, at another in the present. It appears in fact to be a merely formal difference, produced by division of labour and exchange, whether B himself produces the means of subsistence from which he has to exist, or whether he obtains them from A; in which case he does not produce the means of subsistence directly, but produces a suit of clothes instead, for which he receives in exchange, from A, the means of subsistence. In both cases he can only obtain control of the use value possessed by A so long as he gives him an equivalent for it, which in the last resort always comes down to his own living labour, whatever objective form it may assume either before or after the conclusion of the exchange. The suit now not only contains labour which gives it a definite form – a definite form of utility given to the cloth by the movement of labour – but it contains a definite quantity of labour and thus not only use value, but value in general, value as such. But this value does not exist for A, since he has consumed the suit and is not himself a dealer in clothes. He has, therefore, traded in the labour, not as labour which has value, but as something useful, an activity that creates use value. In the rendering of personal services, this use value is consumed as such, without proceeding beyond the form of activity into that of a material thing. When, as often happens in simple relationships, the person who renders a service does not receive money for it but only immediate use values, the illusion that we are here concerned on

---

[1] ['I give so that you may do.']    [2] ['I do so that you may give.']
[3] ['I give so that you may give.']

either side with values rather than use values at once disappears. But even assuming that A pays money for the services rendered, this is not a transformation of his money into capital, but indicates that it has been made a mere means of circulation, in order to obtain an item of consumption, a particular use value. This act is thus not concerned with the production of wealth, but vice versa, it is an act that consumes wealth. What matters to A is not that labour, as such, definite working time, i.e. value, is objectified in the cloth, but that it satisfies a definite need. A's money is not valorised but de-valorised, during the process of converting it from the form of value into that of use value. Labour is here exchanged not as use value for the value, but as a special use value, as value for use. The more frequently A repeats the exchange, the more impoverished he becomes. This type of exchange is not an act of enrichment for him, nor an act of value creation; it is a devalorisation of values that exist and are in his possession. The money that A has exchanged for living labour – either a natural service, or service objectified in a material thing – is not *capital* but revenue. It is money as a means of circulation, in order to obtain use value. Use value has a merely ephemeral form in it, and the money is not used to buy labour which will be retained and valorised. The exchange of *money as revenue*, purely as a means of circulation against living labour, can never establish money as capital, nor labour as wage-labour in the economic sense. There is no need to explain in detail why the consumption or spending of money is not the same thing as producing money. In conditions in which most of the surplus labour is agricultural, and in which the landowner retains both the surplus labour and the surplus product, it is the revenue of the landowner which forms the labour fund for the free worker, the manufacturing worker (we refer here to manufacturing by hand), as opposed to the agricultural worker. This exchange is a form of landowner's consumption; he directly distributes another part of his revenue in return for personal services – often only an illusion of personal service with a lot of retainers. In Asiatic societies, where the monarch is the exclusive proprietor of the surplus product of the land, entire towns exist which are basically nothing more than nomadic camps, because of the exchange of his revenue with 'free hands', as Steuart terms them. In this relationship there is no wage-labour, although it may (it need not) come into contradiction with slavery and bondage, since it is always found in the most diverse forms of social organisation. In so far as money arranges this exchange, the fixing of prices is important for both sides (but for A only in so far as he does not wish to pay too highly for the use value of the labour; and not because he is concerned with its value). It makes no essential difference that originally this price is chiefly conventional and traditional; and then little by little becomes determined first economically, according to supply and demand, and later by the costs of production, whereby those who sell these living services can themselves be produced. For both before and after, the price-fixing remains only a formal element in the exchange of pure use values. This price is fixed by other relationships, viz. the general laws in force determined by the dominant means of production, and operating behind such particular acts of exchange. In the ancient world, one of the entities in which this type of remuneration first appeared was the army. The ordinary soldier's pay was kept down to a minimum – it was determined solely by the production costs involved in producing soldiers. But the services rendered by the soldier were paid for out of state revenue, not from capital.

In bourgeois society, all forms of exchange of personal service for revenue come under this heading – from labour for personal consumption (the labour of the cook, the seamstress, the gardener) up to the work performed by all the generally non-productive classes – state employees, doctors, lawyers, teachers, etc., also all menial servants, etc. All these workers, from the humblest to the highest, negotiate the exchange of their services (often compulsory) against a part of the surplus product, against the capitalist's revenue. But no one would ever think that the capitalist, by exchanging his revenue for this kind of personal service – that is, by privately consuming it – sets himself up as a capitalist; rather, he is spending the fruits of his capital. The fact that the proportions in which revenue is exchanged for this living labour are themselves determined by the general laws of production does not alter the nature of the relationship.

As we pointed out in the section on money, it is rather the provider of services who establishes value, converting a use value (a definite kind of labour or service) into value, money. So, in the

Middle Ages, the production and accumulation of money started from living labour partly in opposition to landowning nobility who were the consumers. To a certain extent, it was the emancipated bondmen who accumulated money and would later become the capitalists.

It is not the general relationship that determines whether the provider of services receives a salary, a daily wage or a professional fee, or a civil list pension, or whether his rank is superior or inferior to that of the person paying for the service; this depends on the natural, particular quality of the service rendered. Once capital has established itself as the dominating force, all such relationships are in any case more or less *dishonoured*. However, this loss of the semi-divine character of personal service, and the sublime character that tradition may have conferred upon it, cannot be dealt with here.

Capital, and thus wage-labour, is therefore not constituted by a simple exchange of objectified labour for living labour; from this standpoint they are two different forms occurring as use values of different kinds, one in an objective form and the other in a subjective form. For that there must be an exchange of objectified labour that exists as a value for itself against labour as living use value that belongs to it, as use value for value, not for any particular or special use or consumption.

During the exchange of money for labour or service for direct consumption there is always a real exchange. Quantities of labour are exchanged on both sides, though this is only of formal interest, enabling the particular, special utility forms of the labour to be measured. This refers only to the form of the exchange, and does not constitute its content. In the exchange of capital for labour, value is no measurement for the exchange of two use values, but the content of the exchange itself.

2. At the time when pre-bourgeois conditions were dissolved, free workers were seen to appear sporadically whose services were bought not for purposes of consumption but for production. First of all, this took place on a large scale only for the production of immediate use values, not values. Secondly, it occurred when the nobility, for example, employed free workers alongside bondmen, and resold part of the worker's product. Thus the free worker produced value for him; but then only in relation to the super-

fluity, in order to increase superfluous luxury consumption. Basically this is only a disguised purchase of alien labour for direct,
immediate consumption, or as a use value. Besides, in situations
where the free workers were multiplying, so that this relationship
was increasing, the old means of production – communal, patriarchal or feudal – were disintegrating, and the factors that fav-
oured real wage-labour were being prepared. But in Poland, for
example, these free servants may suddenly emerge, and as suddenly disappear, without the means of production being altered.

In order to express the relations that are established between
capital and labour in terms of property relationships or laws, it is
enough to illustrate the behaviour of both sides in the valorisation
process as a process of appropriation. For example the fact that
surplus labour is established as the surplus value of capital means
that the worker does not appropriate the product of his own
labour; that it seems to him to be alien property; or vice versa,
that alien labour appears to be the property of capital. This
second law of bourgeois property, derived from the first and
equally well established, is perpetuated by the law of succession,
etc., which gives it an existence independent of the risks inherent
in the ephemeral life of the individual capitalist. The first pro-
claims the identity of labour and property; the second, labour as
negated property, or property as the negation of the alien nature
of alien labour. In fact, in the production process of capital, as
we shall see when we develop this still further, labour is a totality
– a combination of kinds of labour – of which the individual constituents are alien to each other, so that the total labour is not
the achievement of individual workers, and their product is only
a totality through the enforced combination of efforts that they
cannot themselves co-ordinate. In this combination, labour serves
an alien will and an alien intelligence; it is they who direct it. Its
uniting principle and its soul exist outside labour, and its material
unity is subordinated to the objectified unity of machinery and
to fixed capital. This is the animated monster which objectifies
scientific thought, and in practice unifies the entire process. It
does not behave as the instrument of the individual worker; on
the contrary, the worker, an individual endowed with a soul of
his own, exists as a living, isolated accessory of the system as a
whole. Combined labour is thus doubly a combination in itself;

not a combination which links individuals working together, nor one which transcends either their special, isolated function, or the instrument of labour.

Thus, in that the worker relates to the product of his labour as to something alien, he relates to combined labour also as to something alien, and to his own labour as his own manifestation of life, but alien to him and imposed on him; so that, as A. Smith has said, it is a burden and a sacrifice. Labour itself, like its product, is no longer that of the particular individual worker. It is the negation of individual labour, since labour is now in fact collective or combined labour. This kind of labour, both as activity and in its static form of object, is at the same time established as directly other than the actually existing individual labour. It is at the same time alien objectivity (alien property) and alien subjectivity (that of capital). Thus capital represents the negation both of labour and its product in the individual form, and therefore of the property of the individual worker. It thus exists in the form of collective labour, combined both as subject and object, but independently of its real elements: it has, therefore, a separate existence. Capital is thus the transcendent subject and owner of alien labour, so that its relationship is thus as complete a contradiction as that of wage-labour.

# 15 The Universalist Tendencies Inherent in Capitalism

From *Grundrisse*, pp. 438–40

*Marx outlines, in very abstract terms, the type of society that capitalism has created in contradistinction both to the feudal society that preceded it and to the communist society that will follow it.*

WHILE on the one hand capital must thus seek to pull down every local barrier to commerce, i.e. to exchange, in order to capture the whole world as its market, on the other hand it strives to destroy space by means of time, i.e. to restrict to a minimum the time required for movement from one place to another. The more developed capital is, and thus the more extensive the market through which it circulates and which constitutes the spatial route of its circulation, the more it will aspire to greater extension in space for its market, and thus to greater destruction of space by time. (If working time is not considered as the working day of the individual worker, but as an indeterminate working day of an indeterminate number of workers, all *population relationships* come into this; the basic theory of population is thus also included in this first chapter on capital, in the same way as the theory of profit, price, credit, etc.) We see here the universal tendency of capital which distinguishes it from all earlier stages of production. Although it is itself limited by its own nature, capital strives after the universal development of productive forces, and thus becomes the prerequisite for a new means of production. This means of production is founded not on the development of productive forces in order to reproduce a given condition and, at best, to extend it, but is one where free, uninhibited, progressive and universal development of productive forces itself forms the prerequisite of society and thus of its reproduction; where the only prerequisite is to proceed beyond the point of departure. This tendency – which capital possesses, but which at the same time contradicts it as a limited form of production, and thus impels it towards its own dissolution – distinguishes capital from all earlier means of production, and contains the implication of its own transitory nature. All previous forms of society foundered on the development of wealth – or, which amounts to the same thing, on the development of social productive forces. Therefore ancient philosophers who were aware of this bluntly denounced wealth as destructive of community. The feudal institutions in their turn collapsed under urban industry, trade, modern agriculture (even under individual discoveries, such as gunpowder and the printing-press). With the development of wealth – and of new forces and extended individual trade – the economic conditions upon which the community rested were dissolved. The political relationships corresponding to the different constituents of the community suffered the same fate; as did religion, in which it was seen in an idealised form (and both these rested on a given relationship to nature, into which all productive force can be resolved); and the character and points of view of individual people. The development of science alone – i.e. of the most solid form of wealth, which is both a product of wealth and a producer of it – was sufficient to make this community disintegrate. *The development of science*, of this ideal and at the same time practical wealth, is however only one aspect, one form, of the *development of human productive forces* (i.e. wealth). *Ideally* considered, the disintegration of a particular form of consciousness was enough to kill an entire epoch. In reality, this limitation of consciousness corresponds to a *definite stage of development of material productive forces*, and thus of wealth. Of course, development occurred not only on the old basis; there was development of the basis itself. The highest development of this basis, the point of flowering at which it changes (it is nevertheless still *this* basis, this plant in flower, and therefore it fades after flowering and as a consequence of flowering), is the point at which it has been elaborated to a form in which it can be united with the *highest development of productive* forces, and thus also with the richest development of the individual. As soon as this point has been reached, any further development takes the form of a decline, and any fresh development takes place from a new basis. We saw earlier that ownership of the means of production was identified with a limited, determined form of community and thus also of individuals possessing qualities and a development as limited as those of the community that they form.

This prerequisite itself was, in its turn, the result of a limited historical stage of the development of productive forces, a limitation of wealth, just as much as of the knowledge of how to achieve it. The purpose of this community and of these individuals – as a condition of production – is the *reproduction of these determined conditions of production* and of the individuals who, both as single individuals and in their social differentiations and relations, are the living carriers of these relationships. Capital itself establishes the *production of wealth* as such and hence the universal development of productive forces, the incessant upheaval of the prerequisites present in it, as a prerequisite of its reproduction. Value does not exclude any use value; nor does it include, as an absolute condition, any special kind of consumption or trade. Likewise any stage of development of socially productive forces, trade, science, etc., appears to it only as an obstacle that it seeks to overcome. Its prerequisite itself – value – is established as a product, not as a prerequisite higher than production and transcending it. The limitation of *capital* is that this whole development brings out contradictions, and that the elaboration of productive forces, of general wealth, science, etc., appears in such a form that the working individual alienates himself, relating to the conditions that he has produced not as to the conditions of his own wealth but as to those of alien wealth and his own poverty. But this contradictory form is itself a transitory one, and produces the real conditions of its own termination. The result is the creation of a basis that consists in the tendency towards universal development of the productive forces – and wealth in general, also the universality of commerce and a world market. The basis offers the possibility of the universal development of individuals, and the real development of individuals from this basis consists in the constant abolition of each limitation once it is conceived of *as* a limitation and not as a sacred boundary. The universality of the individual is not thought or imagined, but is the universality of his real and ideal relationships. Man therefore becomes able to understand his own history as a *process*, and to conceive of nature (involving also practical control over it) as his own real body. The process of development is itself established and understood as a prerequisite. But it is necessary also and above all that full development of the productive forces should have become a *condition of production*, not that determined *conditions of production* should be set up as a boundary beyond which productive forces cannot develop.

# 16 Labour as Sacrifice or Self-realisation

From *Grundrisse*, pp. 504–8

*Marx here comments at length on Adam Smith's negative attitude to work as being always a burden. In this extract Marx presents a different picture of work as the fulfilment of man's most profound capacities. He also attacks Smith on the ground that the price of goods cannot be determined by labour if labour is viewed solely as a sacrifice.*

A. Smith's view is that labour never changes its value, in the sense that a determined quantity of labour is always a determined quantity for the worker, i.e. according to A. Smith, it is a sacrifice which is quantitatively of an equal size. Whether I receive more or less money for an hour's work (depending on its productivity and other circumstances), I have worked for one hour. What I have had to pay for the result of my labour, for my wages, is always the same hour of working time, no matter how variable its result. 'Equal quantities of labour, at all times and places, may be said to be of equal value to the labourer. In his ordinary state of health, strength and spirits; in the ordinary degree of his skill and dexterity, he must always lay down the same portion of his ease, his liberty, and his happiness. The price which he pays must always be the same, whatever may be the quantity of goods which he receives in return for it. Of these, indeed, it may sometimes purchase a greater and sometimes a smaller quantity; but it is their value which varies, not that of the labour which purchases them. . . . Labour alone, therefore, never varying in its own value, is alone the ultimate and real standard by which the value of all commodities can at all times and places be estimated and compared. It is their real price; money is their nominal price only.'[1] 'Thou shalt labour by the sweat of thy brow!' was Jehovah's

[1] A. Smith, *The Wealth of Nations*, ed. E. Cannan (London, 1904) p. 37.

curse that he bestowed upon Adam. A. Smith conceives of labour
as such a curse. 'Rest' appears to him to be the fitting state of
things, and identical with 'liberty' and 'happiness'. It seems to be
far from A. Smith's thoughts that the individual, 'in his normal
state of health, strength, activity, skill and efficiency', might also
require a normal portion of work, and of cessation from rest. It is
true that the quantity of labour to be provided seems to be conditioned by external circumstances, by the purpose to be achieved,
and the obstacles to its achievement that have to be overcome by
labour. But neither does it occur to A. Smith that the overcoming
of such obstacles may itself constitute an exercise in liberty, and
that these external purposes lose their character of mere natural
necessities and are established as purposes which the individual
himself fixes. The result is the self-realisation and objectification
of the subject, therefore real freedom, whose activity is precisely
labour. Of course he is correct in saying that labour has always
seemed to be repulsive, and forced upon the worker from outside,
in its historical forms of slave-labour, bond-labour and wage-
labour, and that in this sense non-labour could be opposed to
it as 'liberty and happiness'. This is doubly true of this contradictory labour which has not yet created the subjective and objective
conditions (which it lost when it abandoned pastoral conditions)
which make it into attractive labour and individual self-realisation. This does not mean that labour can be made merely a joke,
or amusement, as Fourier naïvely expressed it in shop-girl terms.
Really free labour, the composing of music for example, is at the
same time damned serious and demands the greatest effort. The
labour concerned with material production can only have this
character if (1) it is of a social nature, (2) it has a scientific character and at the same time is general work, i.e. if it ceases to be
human effort as a definite, trained natural force, gives up its
purely natural, primitive aspects and becomes the activity of a
subject controlling all the forces of nature in the production
process. Moreover, A. Smith is thinking only of the slaves of
capital. For example, even the semi-artistic worker of the Middle
Ages cannot be included in his definition. However, my immediate
concern is not to discuss his philosophic view of labour, but only
its economic aspect. Labour considered purely as a sacrifice and
therefore as establishing a value, labour as the price to be paid

for things and thus giving them a price according as they cost
more or less labour, is a purely negative definition. In this way
Mr Senior was able, for example, to make capital into a source of
production *sui generis* in the same sense as labour a source of
production of value, since the capitalist too is making a sacrifice,
the sacrifice of abstinence, for, instead of directly consuming his
produce, he is enriching himself. A pure negative accomplishes
nothing. When the worker takes pleasure in his work – as, certainly, Senior's miser takes pleasure in his abstinence – the product loses nothing of its value. It is labour alone that produces;
it is the only substance of products considered as values.[1] This
is why working time (supposing it is of the same intensity) is the
measure of value. The qualitative differences among workers – in
so far as they are not the natural ones of sex, age, physical
strength, etc., and express, fundamentally, not the qualitative
value of labour, but its division and differentiation – are the result
of historical processes. For the great majority of workers, these
differences disappear again, since the work that they perform is
simple; work that is of a higher quality, however, can be measured
by economics in terms of simple labour. To say that working time,
or the quantity of labour, measures values, means only that labour
and values are measured by the same standard. Two things can
only be measured by the same standard when they are of the same
nature. Therefore products can only be measured by the standard
of labour (working time) because they are by nature made from
labour. They are objectified labour. As objects they may assume
forms that show they were produced by labour and that finality
has been imposed on them from the outside. This does not always

[1] Proudhon's axiom that all work leaves a surplus shows how little he
understands the position. What he denies to capital, he allows to be a natural
property of labour. The point is rather that the working time necessary for
the satisfaction of absolute necessities leaves some free time (which varies at
the various stages of the development of the productive forces), so that surplus produce can thus be created if surplus labour is done. The object is to
terminate this relationship, so that surplus produce itself can become necessary, and finally material production can leave everyone surplus time for other
activities. There is no longer anything mystical about this. Originally the
spontaneously developing association (the family) existed at the beginning
together with a corresponding division of labour and co-operation. But then
needs were slight in the beginning, and only developed with the productive
forces. [Marx's footnote.]

occur; it is not possible to see objectified labour in an ox, nor in the products of nature that man reproduces. These forms, however, have nothing in common with each other; they exist as something constant so long as they have an existence as an activity measured by time, which can thus also be used to measure objectified labour. We shall examine later how far this measurement is linked to exchange, and to labour that is not yet socially organised, as a definite stage of the social productive process. Use value is not connected with human activity as the source and creation of the product, it aims at producing an object that is useful for man. In so far as the product has a measure of its own, it is measured in terms of its natural properties – size, weight, length, capacity, measure of usefulness, etc. But as an effect, or as the static form of the force that has created it, it is measured only by the volume of this force itself. The measure of labour is time. Simply because products *are* labour, they can be measured by the measure of labour, by the working time, or the quantity of labour consumed in them. The negation of rest, as a pure negation, as an ascetic sacrifice, accomplishes nothing. An individual may mortify the flesh and make a martyr of himself from morning to night, like the monks, but the amount of sacrifice that he makes will get him nowhere. The natural price of things is not the sacrifice made to obtain them. This is reminiscent of the pre-industrial era, in which riches were to be obtained by sacrifices to the gods. There must be something else besides the sacrifice. Instead of speaking of a sacrifice of rest, one might speak of a sacrifice of laziness, of lack of freedom, of unhappiness – in fact, the negation of a negative condition. A. Smith considers labour from the psychological point of view, in relation to the pleasure or opposite that it gives to the individual. But in addition to being a feeling concerning his activity, work is something else: in the first place, in relationship to other people, for the mere sacrifice of A would be no use to B. Secondly, there is the worker's own particular relationship towards the object that he is making, and towards his own talents for work. Work is a positive, creative activity. The standard by which work is measured – i.e. time – naturally does not depend on its productivity. The measure consists of a unity, whose aliquot parts express a certain quantity. It certainly does not follow from this that the value of labour is constant; it is so only in so far as equal quantities of labour have the same unity of measurement. Pursuing this analysis further, we find that the values of products are measured by labour, not the labour actually employed, but the labour that is necessary for their production. Thus the condition of production is not the sacrifice but the labour. The equation expresses the condition of its reproduction given in the exchange, in other words, the possibility of renewing productive activity created by its own product.

Moreover, if A. Smith's idea of sacrifice correctly expresses the subjective relationship of the wage-earner to his own work, it still will not yield what he wishes it to – namely, that value is determined by means of the time worked. From the worker's point of view, even one hour of work may represent a great sacrifice. But the value of his work does not in the slightest depend on his feelings; nor does the value of the hour he has worked. A. Smith admits that this sacrifice may sometimes be bought more cheaply, sometimes more dearly; in which case one is struck by the fact that it must always be sold at the same price. In this also he is illogical. Further on, he declares wages to be the standard by which value is measured, not the quantity of labour. To go to the slaughter is always the same sacrifice for the ox; this is no reason for beef to have a constant value.

# 17 Individual Freedom in Capitalist Society

From *Grundrisse*, pp. 542–5

*Marx once again describes the genesis of capitalism and gives the most extensive critique of capitalist freedom to be found in the* Grundrisse. *According to Marx, the type of freedom to be found in bourgeois society is by no means absolute, but as limited as that of any previous society. Moreover, it will disappear with the transcendence of capitalist society.*

HISTORICALLY, competition meant the abolition of guild coercion, governmental regulations, and the abolition of frontiers, tolls, etc., within a state – and in the world market it meant the abolition of tariffs, protection and prohibition. In short, it was historically a negation of the limits and obstacles peculiar to the levels of production that obtained before the development of capital. These were described quite correctly, historically speaking, by the physiocrats as *laissez faire, laissez passer,* and advocated by them as such. Competition, however, has never been considered from the purely negative and purely historical aspect; indeed even more stupid interpretations have been put forward, for example that competition represents the clash between individuals released from their chains and acting only in their own interests; or that it represents the repulsion and attraction of free individuals in relation to one another, and thus is the absolute form of individual liberty in the sphere of production and exchange. Nothing could be more wrong.

Although free competition has abolished the obstacles created by the relationships and means of pre-capitalist production, it should first be remembered that what were restrictions for capital were inherent frontiers for earlier means of production, within which they developed and moved naturally. These frontiers became obstacles only after productive forces and commercial relationships had sufficiently developed for capital to be the ruling principle of production. The frontiers that it tore down were obstacles to its own movement, development and realisation. It did not abolish all frontiers by any means, or all obstacles; only those that did not correspond to its needs, those that were obstacles for it. Within its own limitations – however much these may seem, from a higher point of view, to be obstacles in production, and have been fixed as such by the historical development of capital – it feels itself free and unhampered, that is, bounded only by itself, but its own conditions of existence.

In the same way the industry of the guilds in its heyday found that the guild organisation gave it the freedom it needed, i.e. the production relationships corresponding to it. Guild industry gave rise to these relationships, developing them as its own inherent conditions, and thus not at all as external, restricting obstacles. The historical aspect of the negation of guild industry, etc., by capital, by means of free competition, means nothing more than that capital, sufficiently strengthened by a means of circulation adequate for its nature, tore down the historical barriers which interfered with and restricted its movement. But competition is far removed from possessing merely this historical significance, or from playing merely this negative role. *Free competition* is the relation of capital to itself as another capital, i.e. it is the real behaviour of capital as such. It is only then that the internal laws of capital – which appear only as tendencies in the early historical stages of its evolution – can be established; production founded on capital only establishes itself in so far as free competition develops, since free competition is the free development of the conditions and means of production founded on capital and of the process which constantly reproduces these conditions. It is not individuals but capital that establishes itself freely in free competition. So long as production founded on capital is the necessary and therefore the most suitable form in which social productive forces can develop, the movement of individuals within the pure conditions of capital will seem to be free. This liberty is then assured dogmatically by constant reference to the barriers that have been torn down by free competition. Free competition expresses the real development of capital. Because of it, individual capital finds imposed upon itself an external necessity that

corresponds to the nature of capital, to the means of production
founded on it, to the concept of capital. The mutual constraint
that different portions of capital impose on each other, on labour,
etc. (the competition of workers between themselves is only
another form of the competition of capital), is the *free* and at the
same time the *real* development of wealth as capital. So much so,
that the profoundest economic theorists, Ricardo for example,
begin by *presuming* the absolute domination of free competition,
in order to study and formulate the laws that are suitable to
capital, laws which at the same time appear as the vital tendencies that dominate it. Free competition, however, is the form
suitable to the productive process of capital. The more it develops,
the more clearly the shape of its movement is seen. What Ricardo,
for example, has thus recognised (despite himself) is the historical
nature of capital, and the limited character of free competition,
which is still only the free movement of portions of capital, i.e.
their movement within conditions that have nothing in common
with those of any dissolved preliminary stages, but are their own
conditions. The domination of capital is the prerequisite of free
competition, just as the despotism of the Roman emperors was
the prerequisite of the free Roman civil law. So long as capital is
weak, it will rely on crutches taken from past means of production
or from means of production that are disappearing as it comes
onto the scene. As soon as it feels strong, it throws the crutches
away and moves according to its own laws. As soon as it begins to
feel and to be aware that it is itself an obstacle to development,
it takes refuge in forms that, although they appear to complete
the mastery of capital, are at the same time, by curbing free
competition, the heralds of its dissolution, and of the dissolution
of the means of production which are based on it. What lies in the
nature of capital is only expressed in reality as an external necessity through competition, which means no more than that the
various portions of capital impose the inherent conditions of
capital on one another and on themselves. No category of the
bourgeois economy – not even the first one, the determination of
value – can become real by means of free competition, i.e. through
the real process of capital, which appears as the interaction of
portions of capital on one another and of all the other relationships of production and circulation that are determined by capital.

Hence the absurdity of considering free competition as being the final development of human liberty, and the negation of free competition as being the negation of individual liberty and of social production founded on individual liberty. It is only free development on a limited foundation — that of the dominion of capital. This kind of individual liberty is thus at the same time the most complete suppression of all individual liberty and total subjugation of individuality to social conditions which take the form of material forces — and even of all-powerful objects that are independent of the individuals relating to them. The only rational answer to the deification of free competition by the middle-class prophets, or its diabolisation by the socialists, lies in its own development. If it is said that, within the limits of free competition, individuals by following their pure self-interest realise their social, or rather their general, interest, this means merely that they exert pressure upon one another under the conditions of capitalist production and that this clash between them can only give rise to the conditions under which their interaction took place. Moreover, once the illusion that competition is the supposedly absolute form of free individuality disappears, this proves that the conditions of competition, i.e. of production founded on capital, are already felt and thought of as a barrier, that they indeed already are such and will increasingly become so. The assertion that free competition is the final form of the development of productive forces, and thus of human freedom, means only that the domination of the middle class is the end of the world's history — of course quite a pleasant thought for yesterday's parvenus!

# 18 The Labour Process and Alienation in Machinery and Science

From *Grundrisse*, pp. 583–92

*In this passage Marx extrapolates tendencies inherent in his own time and foresees automation and technology as major factors in man's alienation; but he sees them equally as factors bringing about the collapse of capitalism and the transition to a future communist society.*

So long as the means of labour remains a means of labour, in the proper sense of the word, as it has been directly and historically assimilated by capital into its valorisation process, it only undergoes a formal change, in that it appears to be the means of labour not only from its material aspect, but at the same time as a special mode of existence of capital determined by the general process of capital – it has become *fixed capital*. But once absorbed into the production process of capital, the means of labour undergoes various metamorphoses, of which the last is the *machine*, or rather, an *automatic system of machinery* ('automatic' meaning that this is only the most perfected and most fitting form of the machine, and is what transforms the machinery into a system).

This is set in motion by an automaton, a motive force that moves of its own accord. The automaton consists of a number of mechanical and intellectual organs, so that the workers themselves can be no more than the conscious limbs of the automaton. In the machine and still more in machinery as an automatic system, the means of labour is transformed as regards its use value, i.e. as regards its material existence, into an existence suitable for fixed capital and capital in general; and the form in which it was assimilated as a direct means of labour into the production process of capital is transformed into one imposed by capital itself and in accordance with it. In no respect is the machine the means of labour of the individual worker. Its distinctive character is not at all, as with the means of labour, that of transmitting the activity of the worker to its object; rather this activity is so arranged that it now only transmits and supervises and protects from damage the work of the machine and its action on the raw material.

With the tool it was quite the contrary. The worker animated it with his own skill and activity; his manipulation of it depended on his dexterity. The machine, which possesses skill and force in the worker's place, is itself the virtuoso, with a spirit of its own in the mechanical laws that take effect in it; and, just as the worker consumes food, so the machine consumes coal, oil, etc. (instrumental material), for its own constant self-propulsion. The worker's activity, limited to a mere abstraction, is determined and regulated on all sides by the movement of the machinery, not the other way round. The knowledge that obliges the inanimate parts of the machine, through their construction, to work appropriately as an automaton, does not exist in the consciousness of the worker, but acts upon him through the machine as an alien force, as the power of the machine itself. The appropriation of living labour by objectified labour – of valorising strength or activity by self-sufficient value – which is inherent in the concept of capital, is established as the character of the production process itself – when production is based on machinery – as a function of its material elements and material movement. The production process has ceased to be a labour process in the sense that labour is no longer the unity dominating and transcending it. Rather labour appears merely to be a conscious organ, composed of individual living workers at a number of points in the mechanical system; dispersed, subjected to the general process of the machinery itself, it is itself only a limb of the system, whose unity exists not in the living workers but in the living (active) machinery, which seems to be a powerful organism when compared to their individual, insignificant activities. With the stage of machinery, objectified labour appears in the labour process itself as the dominating force opposed to living labour, a force represented by capital in so far as it appropriates living labour.

That the labour process is no more than a simple element in the valorisation process is confirmed by the transformation on the material plane of the working tool into machinery, and of the living worker into a mere living accessory of the machine; they become no more than the means whereby its action can take place.

As we have seen, capital necessarily tends towards an increase in the productivity of labour and as great a diminution as possible in necessary labour. This tendency is realised by means of the transformation of the instrument of labour into the machine. In machinery, objectified labour is materially opposed to living labour as its own dominating force; it subordinates living labour to itself not only by appropriating it, but in the real process of production itself. The character of capital as value that appropriates value-creating activity is established by fixed capital, existing as machinery, in its relationship as the use value of labour power. Further, the value objectified in machinery appears as a prerequisite, opposed to which the valorising power of the individual worker disappears, since it has become infinitely small.

In the large-scale production created by machines, any relationship of the product to the direct requirements of the producer disappears, as does any immediate use value. The form of production, and the circumstances in which production takes place are so arranged that it is only produced as a vehicle for value, its use value being only a condition for this.

In machinery, objectified labour appears not only in the form of a product, or of a product utilised as a means of labour, but also in the force of production itself. The development of the means of labour into machinery is not fortuitous for capital; it is the historical transformation of the traditional means of labour into means adequate for capitalism. The accumulation of knowledge and skill, of the general productive power of society's intelligence, is thus absorbed into capital in opposition to labour and appears as the property of capital, or more exactly of fixed capital, to the extent that it enters into the production process as an actual means of production. Thus machinery appears as the *most adequate form of fixed capital;* and the latter, in so far as capital can be considered as being related to itself, is the most adequate form of capital in general. On the other hand, in so far as fixed capital is firmly tied to its existence as a particular use value, it no longer corresponds to the concept of capital which, as a value, can take up or throw off any particular form of use value, and incarnate itself in any of them indifferently. Seen from this aspect of the external relationships of capital, *circulating capital* seems to be the most adequate form of capital as opposed to fixed capital.

In so far as machinery develops with the accumulation of social knowledge and productive power generally, it is not in labour but in capital that general social labour is represented. Society's productivity is measured in fixed capital, exists within it in an objectified form; and conversely, the productivity of capital evolves in step with this general progress that capital appropriates gratis. We shall not go into the development of machinery in detail here. We are considering it only from the general aspect, to the extent that the means of labour, in its material aspect, loses its immediate form and opposes the worker materially as capital. Science thus appears, in the machine, as something alien and exterior to the worker; and living labour is subsumed under objectified labour, which acts independently. The worker appears to be superfluous in so far as his action is not determined by the needs of capital.

Thus the full development of capital does not take place – in other words, capital has not set up the means of production corresponding to itself – until the means of labour is not only formally determined as fixed capital, but has been transcended in its direct form, and fixed capital in the shape of a machine is opposed to labour within the production process. The production process as a whole, however, is not subordinated to the direct skill of the worker; it has become a technological application of science.

The tendency of capital is thus to give a scientific character to production, reducing direct labour to a simple element in this process. As with the transformation of value into capital, we see when we examine the development of capital more closely that on the one hand it presupposes a definite historical development of the productive forces (science being included among these forces), and on the other hand accelerates and compels this development.

The quantitative volume, and the efficiency (intensity) with which capital develops as fixed capital, thus shows in general the degree to which capital has developed as capital, as domination over living labour, and the degree to which it dominates the production process in general. It also expresses the accumulation of objectified productive forces and likewise of objectified labour.

But if capital only adequately displays its nature as use value within the production process in the form of machinery and other material forms of fixed capital, railways, for example (we shall return to this later), this never means that this use value (machinery by itself) *is* capital, or that machinery can be regarded as synonymous with capital; any more than gold would cease to have usefulness as gold, if it were no longer used as money. Machinery does not lose its use value when it ceases to be capital. From the fact that machinery is the most suitable form of the use value of fixed capital, it does not follow that its subordination to the social relations of capitalism is the most suitable and final social production relationship for the utilisation of machinery.

To the same degree that working time – the mere quantity of labour – is established by capital as the sole determining element, direct labour and its quantity cease to be the determining element in production and thus in the creation of use value. It is reduced quantitatively to a smaller proportion, just as qualitatively it is reduced to an indispensable but subordinate role as compared with scientific labour in general, the technological application of the natural sciences, and the general productive forces arising from the social organisation of production. This force appears to be a natural gift of community labour, although it is a historical product. In this way capital works for its own dissolution as the dominant form of production.

The transformation of the process of production from the simple labour process into a scientific process, which subjects the forces of nature and converts them to the service of human needs, appears to be a property of fixed capital as opposed to living labour. Individual labour ceases altogether to be productive as such; or rather, it is productive only in collective labour, which subjects the forces of nature. This promotion of immediate labour to the level of community labour shows that individual work is reduced to helplessness vis-à-vis the concentration of common interest represented in capital. On the other hand, a property of *circulating capital* is the retention of labour in one branch of production thanks to coexisting labour in another branch.

In small-scale circulation, capital advances the worker his wages, which he exchanges for products necessary for his own consumption. The money that he receives only has this power because, at the same time, work is being carried out alongside him. It is only because capital has appropriated his labour that it can give him, with the money, control over the labour of others. This exchange of the worker's own labour for that of others does not seem to be determined and conditioned by the simultaneous co-existence of the others' labour, but by the advance that capital has made to him.

It appears to be a property of the part of the *circulating capital* that is assigned to the worker, and of circulating capital in general, that the worker can proceed to the assimilation of what he himself needs during the process of production. This exchange appears as the material exchange not of simultaneous forces, but of capital; because of the existence of circulating capital. Thus all the forces of labour are transposed into forces of capital; in its fixed part, the productive force of labour (which is placed outside it and exists materially independently of it); and in its circulating part, we find first of all that the worker has himself produced the conditions for the renewal of his work, and secondly that the exchange of his labour is mediated through the coexisting labour of others in such a way that capital appears to make him the advance and to ensure the existence of labour in other branches. (Both the latter statements really belong to the chapter on accumulation.) Capital sets itself up as a mediator between the various labourers in the form of circulating capital.

Fixed capital, considered as a means of production, whose most adequate form is machinery, only produces value (i.e. increases the value of the product) in two cases: (1) in so far as it has value, i.e. in so far as it is itself the product of labour, a definite quantity of labour in an objectified form; (2) in so far as it increases the proportion of surplus labour to necessary labour by making it possible for labour, by increasing its productivity, to create more quickly a larger amount of the products needed for the sustenance of living labour power. To say that the worker is in co-operation with the capitalist because the latter makes the worker's labour easier by means of fixed capital, or shortens his labour, is a bourgeois phrase of the greatest absurdity. Fixed capital is in any case the product of labour, and is merely alien labour that has been appropriated by capital; and the capitalist could be said, rather, to be robbing labour of all its independent and attractive character by means of the machine. On the contrary, capital only uses machinery in so far as it enables the worker to devote more of his working time to the capitalist, to work longer for others and experience a larger part of his time as not belonging to him. Through this process, in fact, the quantity of labour necessary for the production of a particular object is reduced to a minimum, so that a maximum of labour can be valorised into the maximum number of such objects. The first aspect is important, because capital in this instance has quite unintentionally reduced human labour, the expenditure of energy, to a minimum. This will be to the advantage of emancipated labour, and is the condition of its emancipation.

All this shows the absurdity of Lauderdale's statement that fixed capital is independent of working time, and a self-contained source of value.[1] It is such a source only in so far as it is itself objectified labour time, and establishes surplus labour time. The introduction of machines historically presupposes superfluous hands. Machinery only replaces labour when there is a superfluity of labour force. Only in the imagination of economists does it come to the aid of the individual worker. It can only take effect with masses of workers, whose concentration as opposed to capital is one of its historical prerequisites, as we have seen. It does not arise in order to replace deficient labour power, but to reduce the mass of labour available to the necessary quantity. Only when labour power is present *en masse* is machinery introduced. (We shall return to this later.)

Lauderdale thinks he has made a great discovery when he says that machinery does not increase the productive power of labour but replaces it, or does what labour is unable to do by its own power. It is inherent in the concept of capital that the greater productive power of labour is seen as an increase of a force external to labour and as the enfeeblement of labour itself. The tools of labour make the worker independent – establish him as a proprietor. Machinery – as fixed capital – makes him dependent, expropriates him. Machinery only produces this effect to the extent that it is fixed capital, and it only has this character so long as the worker is related to the machine as a wage-earner, and the active individual in general as a mere worker.

[1] [Cf. James Maitland, Earl of Lauderdale, *An Inquiry into the Nature and Origin of Public Health* (1804).]

Up to this point, fixed and circulating capital have appeared to be merely different, transitory determinations of capital; but now they are crystallised into special forms of existence of capital and circulating capital occurs alongside fixed capital. There are now two different kinds of capital. If we consider capital in a particular branch of production we see that it is divided into two parts, or that it is divided in a determined proportion into these two kinds of capital.

The difference within the production process – originally between the means of labour and labour material, and finally the product of labour – now appears as that between circulating capital (the first two) and fixed capital. The division of capital in its purely material aspect is now assimilated into its own form, which appears as what makes the distinction.

The mistake of such writers as Lauderdale, who state that capital, as such and independently of labour, creates *value*, and thus also *surplus value* (or profit), arises from their superficial view of the matter. Fixed capital, whose material form or use value is machinery, gives most appearance of truth to their fallacies. But against this, e.g. in *Labour Defended*, we see that the constructor of a road is willing to share it with the road user, but that the road itself cannot do this.[1]

Circulating capital – provided only that it proceeds through its various stages – may decrease or increase, shorten or lengthen the circulation time, make the various stages of capitalist circulation easier or more difficult. Consequently, the surplus value that may be produced within a given time may be diminished without these interruptions – either because the number of reproductions is smaller, or because the quantity of capital constantly engaged in the process of production has contracted. In both cases there is no diminution of the presupposed value, but a decrease in its rate of growth.

As we have noted, the extent to which fixed capital has developed is a measure of the development of heavy industry in general, and as soon as it has developed to a certain point, and thus has increased relative to the development of its productive forces (it being itself the objectification of these productive forces

---

[1] [Cf. Thomas Hodgskin, *Labour Defended Against the Claims of Capital* (London, 1825).]

and their presupposed product), from this point onwards any interruption of the process of production will cause a diminution of capital itself and its presupposed value. The value of fixed capital is only reproduced to the extent that it is used up in the production process. If it is not used, it loses its use value without its value being transferred to the product. Thus the more fixed capital develops on a large scale, in the sense in which we have been considering it, the more the continuity of the production process or the constant flow of reproduction will become a condition and an external form of coercion of the means of production founded on capitalism.

From this standpoint, too, the appropriation of living labour by capital is directly expressed in machinery. It is a scientifically based analysis, together with the application of mechanical and chemical laws, that enables the machine to carry out the work formerly done by the worker himself. The development of machinery only follows this path, however, once heavy industry has reached an advanced stage, and the various sciences have been pressed into the service of capital, and, on the other hand, when machinery itself has yielded very considerable resources. Invention then becomes a branch of business, and the application of science to immediate production aims at determining the inventions at the same time as it solicits them. But this is not the way in which machinery in general came into being, still less the way that it progresses in detail. This way is a process of analysis – by subdivision of labour, which transforms the worker's operations more and more into mechanical operations, so that, at a certain point, the mechanism can step into his place.

Thus we can see directly here how a particular means of labour is transferred from the worker to capital in the form of the machine and his own labour power devalued as a result of this transposition. Hence we have the struggle of the worker against machinery. What used to be the activity of the living worker has become that of the machine.

Thus the appropriation of his labour by capital is bluntly and brutally presented to the worker: capital assimilates living labour into itself 'as though love possessed its body'.[1]

[1] [Quotation from Goethe's *Faust*.]

# 19 The Position of Labour in Capitalist and Communist Society

From *Grundrisse*, pp. 592–4

*Marx here describes the inevitable collapse of capitalism due to the introduction of machinery which will create an increasing disproportion between necessary labour time and surplus labour time. Marx then describes the development of the 'social individual' as the aim of communist society. The account that he gives here of the bases of communist society serves as a complement to the well-known account in the* Communist Manifesto *and the* Critique of the Gotha Programme.

THE exchange of living labour for objectified labour, i.e. the establishment of social labour in the antagonistic form of capital and wage-labour, is the final development of the value relationship and of production based on value. The prerequisite for this relationship is the mass of direct labour time, the quantity of labour utilised, which is the decisive factor in the production of wealth. But as heavy industry develops, the creation of real wealth depends less on labour time and on the quantity of labour utilised than on the power of mechanical agents which are set in motion during labour time. The powerful effectiveness of these agents, in its turn, bears no relation to the immediate labour time that their production costs. It depends rather on the general state of science and on technological progress, or the application of this science to production. (The development of science – especially of the natural sciences and with them of all the others – is itself once more related to the development of material production.) Agriculture, for example, is a pure application of the science of material metabolism, and the most advantageous way of employing it for the good of society as a whole.

Real wealth develops much more (as is disclosed by heavy industry) in the enormous disproportion between the labour time utilised and its product, and also in the qualitative disproportion between labour that has been reduced to a mere abstraction, and the power of the production process that it supervises. Labour does not seem any more to be an essential part of the process of production. The human factor is restricted to watching and supervising the production process. (This applies not only to machinery, but also to the combination of human activities and the development of human commerce.)

The worker no longer inserts transformed natural objects as intermediaries between the material and himself; he now inserts the natural process that he has transformed into an industrial one between himself and inorganic nature, over which he has achieved mastery. He is no longer the principal agent of the production process: he exists alongside it. In this transformation, what appears as the mainstay of production and wealth is neither the immediate labour performed by the worker, nor the time that he works – but the appropriation by man of his own general productive force, his understanding of nature and the mastery of it; in a word, the development of the social individual. The theft of others' labour time upon which wealth depends today seems to be a miserable basis compared with this newly developed foundation that has been created by heavy industry itself. As soon as labour, in its direct form, has ceased to be the main source of wealth, then labour time ceases, and must cease, to be its standard of measurement, and thus exchange value must cease to be the measurement of use value. The surplus labour of the masses has ceased to be a condition for the development of wealth in general; in the same way that the non-labour of the few has ceased to be a condition for the development of the general powers of the human mind. Production based on exchange value therefore falls apart, and the immediate process of material production finds itself stripped of its impoverished, antagonistic form. Individuals are then in a position to develop freely. It is no longer a question of reducing the necessary labour time in order to create surplus labour, but of reducing the necessary labour of society to a minimum. The counterpart of this reduction is that all members of society can develop their education in the arts, sciences, etc., thanks to the free time and means available to all.

Capital is itself contradiction in action, since it makes an effort to reduce labour time to the minimum, while at the same time establishing labour time as the sole measurement and source of wealth. Thus it diminishes labour time in its *necessary* form, in order to increase its *superfluous* form; therefore it increasingly establishes superfluous labour time as a condition (a question of life and death) for necessary labour time. On the one hand it calls into life all the forces of science and nature, as well as those of social co-operation and commerce, in order to create wealth which is relatively independent of the labour time utilised. On the other hand it attempts to measure, in terms of labour time, the vast social forces thus created and imprisons them within the narrow limits that are required in order to retain the value already created *as* value. Productive forces and social relationships – the two different sides of the development of the social individual – appear to be, and are, only a *means* for capital, to enable it to produce from its own cramped base. But in fact they are the material conditions that will shatter this foundation.[1]

Nature does not construct machines, locomotives, railways, electric telegraphs, self-acting mules, etc. These are products of human industry; natural material transformed into organs of the human will to dominate nature or to realise itself therein. They are organs of the human brain, created by human hands; the power of knowledge made into an object.

The development of fixed capital shows to what extent general social knowledge has become an immediate productive force, and thus up to what point the conditions for the social life process are themselves subjected to the control of the general intellect, and are remodelled to suit it, and to what extent social productive forces are produced not only in the form of knowledge but also as the direct organs of social practice; of the real life process.

---

[1] 'A nation is truly rich when, instead of working 12 hours, it works only 6. Wealth is not command over surplus labour time' [real wealth], 'but disposable time, beyond that used in immediate production, for each individual and for the whole of society' (*The Source and the Remedy*, etc. (1821) p. 6). [Marx's footnote.]

# 20 Free Time and the Production Process in Capitalist and Communist Society

*From Grundrisse, pp. 595–9*

*Marx gives his account of the changes to be undergone by the production process in communist society and the implications for the worker's time.*

CAPITAL creates a great deal of disposable time, apart from the labour time that is needed for society in general and for each sector of society (i.e. space for the development of the individual's full productive forces, and thus also for those of society). This creation of non-working time is, from the capitalist standpoint, and from that of all earlier stages of development, non-working time or free time for the few. What is new in capital is that it also increases the surplus labour time of the masses by all artistic and scientific means possible, since its wealth consists directly in the appropriation of surplus labour time, since its direct aim is value, not use value. Thus, despite itself, it is instrumental in creating the means of social disposable time, and so in reducing working time for the whole of society to a minimum and thus making everyone's time free for their own development. But although its tendency is always to create disposable time, it also converts it into surplus labour. If it succeeds too well with the former, it will suffer from surplus production, and then the necessary labour will be interrupted as soon as no surplus labour can be valorised from capital. The more this contradiction develops, the clearer it becomes that the growth of productive forces can no longer be limited by the appropriation of the surplus labour of others; the masses of the workers must appropriate their own surplus labour.

When this has been done, disposable time ceases to have a contradictory character. Thus firstly, the labour time necessary will be measured by the requirements of the social individual, and secondly, social productivity will grow so rapidly that, although production is reckoned with a view to the wealth of all, the disposable time of all will increase. For real wealth is the developed productive force of all individuals. It is no longer the labour time but the disposable time which is the measure of wealth. Labour time as the measurement of wealth implies that wealth is founded on poverty, and that disposable time exists in and through opposition to surplus labour time; it implies that all an individual's time is working time, and degrades him to the level of a mere worker, and an instrument of labour. This is why the most developed machinery forces the worker to work longer hours than the savage does, or than the labourer himself when he only had the simplest and most primitive tools to work with.

'If the entire labour of a country were only adequate enough to raise the subsistence of the whole population, there would be no surplus labour, consequently nothing that could be allowed to accumulate as capital. If the people raise in one year enough to support them for two years, one year's consumption must perish, or else men must cease from productive labour for one year. But the possessors of [the] surplus produce or capital . . . employ people upon something not directly and immediately productive, e.g. in the erection of machinery. So it goes on.'[1]

The development of heavy industry means that the basis upon which it rests – the appropriation of the labour time of others – ceases to constitute or to create wealth; and at the same time direct labour as such ceases to be the basis of production, since it is transformed more and more into a supervisory and regulating activity; and also because the product ceases to be made by individual direct labour, and results more from the combination of social activity. 'As the division of labour develops, almost all the work of any individual is a part of the whole, having no value or utility of itself. There is nothing on which the labourer can seize: this is my produce, this I will keep to myself.'[2] In direct exchange between producers, direct individual labour is found to be realised in a particular product, or part of a product, and its common social character – as the objectification of general labour and

[1] [*The Source and the Remedy of the National Difficulties* (London, 1821) (anon.).]

[2] [Hodgskin, *Labour Defended Against the Claims of Capital*, p. 25.]

the satisfaction of general need – is only established through exchange. The opposite takes place in the production process of heavy industry: on the one hand, once the productive forces of the means of labour have reached the level of an automatic process, the prerequisite is the subordination of the natural forces to the intelligence of society, while on the other hand individual labour in its direct form is transformed into social labour. In this way the other basis of this mode of production vanishes.

The labour time used for the production of fixed capital is related, within the production process of capital, to the time used for the production of circulating capital, as surplus labour time to necessary time. To the extent that production directed towards the satisfaction of immediate needs becomes more productive, a larger part of production can be directed towards the satisfaction of the needs of production itself, or the manufacture of means of production. In so far as the production of fixed capital is not materially directed either towards the production of immediate use values, or towards the production of values indispensable for the immediate reproduction of capital – which would again be an indirect representation of use value – but towards the production of means that serve to create value and not towards value as an immediate object; in other words, in so far as fixed capital concentrates on the creation of values and the means of valorisation as the immediate object of production (the production of value is established materially in the object of production itself as the aim of production, the objectification of productive force and the value-producing force of capital) – to that extent it is in the production of fixed capital that capital is established as an end in itself to a more powerful degree than in the production of circulating capital, and becomes effective as capital. Thus, in this sense too, the volume already possessed by fixed capital and the part occupied by its production in general production indicate the standard of development of wealth based on the mode of production of capital.

'The number of workers depends so far on circulating capital, as it depends on the quantity of products of co-existing labour, which labourers are allowed to consume.'[1]

The passages that we have quoted from various economists all

---

[1] [Hodgskin, *Labour Defended Against the Claims of Capital*.]

refer to fixed capital as the part of capital which is included in the production process. 'Flotating capital is consumed; fixed capital is merely used in the great process of production' (*Economist*, vi 1). This is wrong, since it applies only to the part of circulating capital that is itself consumed by fixed capital, by the material instruments. Only fixed capital is consumed 'in the great process of production', considered as the immediate production process.

Consumption within the production process is, however, in fact use. Moreover, neither can the greater durability of fixed capital be understood as a purely material phenomenon. The iron and wood of which my bed is made, the bricks out of which my house is constructed, or the marble statue that adorns a palace, are as durable as the iron and wood that are transformed into machinery. But it is not only for the technical reason that metal, etc., is most often used in machinery that durability is a necessary quality of the instrument and of the means of production, but because the instrument is intended constantly to play the same role in re-peated processes of production. The solidity or durability of the means of production is a direct part of its use value. The more often it has to be renewed, the more expensive it becomes, and the greater the part of capital that must be transformed into it un-profitably. Its durability is thus its existence as a means of pro-duction. Its durability implies an increase in its productivity. With circulating capital on the other hand, if it is not trans-formed into fixed capital, durability does not in any way depend on the productive act itself; and therefore it is not a conceptually established element of it.

'Since the general introduction of soulless machines into British factories, men have been treated, with a few exceptions, as secondary and subordinate machines, and much more attention has been given to the perfecting of raw material made of wood and metals than that made of bodies and minds.'[1]

[1] [Robert Owen, *Essays on the Formation of the Human Character* (London, 1840) p. 31.]

# 21 Leisure and Free Time in Communist Society

From *Grundrisse*, pp. 599–600

*Marx here elaborates on the nature of work in communist society and the possibilities for human development offered by the increase in free time.*

REAL economy – savings – consists in the saving of working time (the minimum, and reduction to the minimum, of production costs); but this saving is identical with the development of productivity. Economising, therefore, does not mean the giving up of pleasure, but the development of power and productive capacity, and thus both the capacity for and the means of enjoyment. The capacity for enjoyment is a condition of enjoyment and therefore its primary means; and this capacity is the development of an individual's talents, and thus of the productive force. To economise on labour time means to increase the amount of free time, i.e. time for the complete development of the individual, which again reacts as the greatest productive force on the productive force of labour. From the standpoint of the immediate production process it may be considered as production of fixed capital; this fixed capital being man himself. It is also self-evident that immediate labour time cannot remain in its abstract contradiction to free time – as in the bourgeois economy. Work cannot become a game, as Fourier would like it to be; his great merit was that he declared that the ultimate object must be to raise to a higher level not distribution but the mode of production. Free time – which includes leisure time as well as time for higher activities – naturally transforms anyone who enjoys it into a different person, and it is this different person who then enters the direct process of production. The man who is being formed finds discipline in this process, while for the man who is already formed it is practice, experimental science, materially creative and self-objectifying knowledge, and he contains within his own head the accumulated wisdom of society. Both of them find exercise in it, to the extent that labour requires practical manipulation and free movement, as in agriculture.

As, little by little, the system of bourgeois economy develops, there develops also its negation, which is its final result. We are now still concerned with the direct process of production. If we consider bourgeois society as a whole, society itself seems to be the final result of the social process of production, i.e. man himself in his relation to society. Everything (such as the product, etc.) which has a fixed form appears only as an element, a vanishing element, in this movement. Even the immediate production process appears here only as an element. The conditions and objectifications of the process are themselves likewise elements of it, the subjects of which are only the individuals, but individuals who are related to one another, in relations which are both reproduced and created anew. It is their own constant process of movement in which they renew both themselves and the world of wealth which they create.

# 22 Productive Power in Capitalist and Communist Society

From *Grundrisse*, pp. 715–17

*Marx here claims that a radically different form of society is possible once the alienated labour of capitalist society has been overcome.*

IT is a fact that as the productive forces of labour develop, the objective conditions of labour (objectified labour) must grow in proportion to living labour. This is actually a tautology, for the growth of the productive forces of labour means merely that less direct labour is required in order to make a larger product, so that social wealth expresses itself more and more in the labour conditions that have been created by labour itself. From the point of view of capital, it does not appear that one of the elements of social activity (objectified labour) has become the ever more powerful body of the other element (subjective, living labour); rather it appears (and this is important for wage-labour) that the objective conditions of labour become more and more colossally independent of living labour – which is shown by their very extent – and social wealth becomes, in ever greater and greater proportions, an alien and dominating force opposing the worker. Stress is placed not on the state of objectification but on the state of alienation, estrangement and abandonment, on the fact that the enormous objectified power which social labour has opposed to itself as one of its elements belongs not to the worker but to the conditions of production that are personified in capital. So long as the creation of this material form of activity, objectified in contrast to immediate labour power, occurs on the basis of capital and wage-labour, and so long as this process of objectification in fact seems to be a process of alienation as far as the worker is concerned, or to be the appropriation of alien labour from the capitalist's point of view, so long will this distortion and this inversion really exist and not merely occur in the imagination of both workers and capitalists. But this process of inversion is obviously merely a historical necessity, a necessity for the development of productive forces from a definite historical starting point, or basis, but in no way an *absolute* necessity of production; it is, rather, ephemeral. The result and the immanent aim of the process is to destroy and transform this basis itself, as well as this form of the process. Bourgeois economists are so bogged down in their traditional ideas of the historical development of society in a single stage that the necessity of the *objectification* of the social forces of labour seems to them inseparable from the necessity of its *alienation* in relation to living labour.

But as living labour loses its *immediate*, individual character, whether subjective or entirely external, as individual activity becomes directly general or *social*, the objective elements of production lose this form of alienation. They are then produced as property, as the organic social body in which individuals are reproduced as individuals, but as social individuals. The conditions for their being such in the reproduction of their life, in their productive life process, can only be established by the historical economic process; these conditions are both objective and subjective conditions, which are the only two different forms of the same conditions.

The fact that the workers possess no property and the fact that objectified labour has property in living labour (in other words, that capital appropriates the labour of others) constitute the two opposite poles of the same relationship, and are the fundamental conditions of the bourgeois means of production and are in no sense a matter of indifference or chance. These means of distribution are the relations of production themselves, but *sub specie distributionis* ('from the point of view of distribution'). Thus it is quite absurd to say, as J. S. Mill does for example (*Principles of Political Economy*, 2nd ed. (London, 1849) I 240), that: 'The laws and conditions of the production of wealth partake of the character of physical truths. . . . It is not so with the distribution of wealth. This is a matter of human institutions solely.' The 'laws and conditions' of the production of wealth and the laws of 'distribution of wealth' are the same laws in a different form; they both change and undergo the same historical process;

they are, in general, never more than elements in a historical process.

No special sagacity is required in order to understand that, beginning with free labour or wage-labour for example, which arose after the abolition of slavery, machines can only develop in opposition to living labour, as a hostile power and alien property, i.e. they must, as capital, oppose the worker. But it is equally easy to see that machines do not cease to be agents of social production, once they become, for example, the property of associated workers. But in the first case, their means of distribution (the fact that they do not belong to the workers) is itself a condition of the means of production that is founded on wage-labour. In the second case, an altered means of distribution will derive from a new, altered basis of production emerging from the historical process.

# Select Bibliography

PREVIOUS EDITIONS

K. Marx, *Grundrisse der Kritik der politischen Oekonomie (Rohentwurf)*, 2 vols (Institute for Marxism-Leninism, Moscow, 1939–41).

K. Marx, *Grundrisse der Kritik der politischen Oekonomie (Rohentwurf)* (Dietz Verlag, Berlin, 1953).

K. Marx, *Texte zu Methode und Praxis*, III, ed. G. Hillmann (Rowohlt, Hamburg, 1966).

K. Marx, *Fondements de la critique de l'économie politique*, trans. R. Dangeville, 2 vols. (Anthropos, Paris, 1967–8).

K. Marx, 'Principes d'une critique de l'économie politique' in M. Rubel (ed.), *Œuvres*, II (Gallimard, Paris, 1968).

K. Marx, *Precapitalist Economic Formations*, ed. E. Hobsbawm (Lawrence & Wishart, London, 1964).


SECONDARY LITERATURE

M. dal Pra, *La dialettica in Marx* (Bari, 1965).

D. Howard, 'On Deforming Marx: The French Translation of *Grundrisse*', *Science and Society* (autumn 1969).

H. Klages, *Technischer Humanismus, Philosophie und Soziologie der Arbeit bei Karl Marx* (Stuttgart, 1964).

E. Mandel, *La Formation de la pensée économique de Karl Marx* (Paris, 1967).

D. McLellan, *Marx before Marxism* (London, and New York 1970).

D. McLellan, 'Marx and the Missing Link', *Encounter* (December 1970).

M. Nicolaus, 'The Unknown Marx', *New Left Review* (April 1968).

B. Ollman, *Alienation: Mark's Concept of Man in Capitalist Society* (Cambridge 1971).

R. Rosdolsky, *Zur Entstehungsgeschichte des Marxschen Kapitals* (Frankfurt, 1968).

M. Rubel, preface to K. Marx, *Œuvres*, II (Paris, 1968).

A. Schmidt, *Der Begriff der Natur in der Lehre von Karl Marx* (Frankfurt, 1962).

# Index

73 10 9 8 7 6 5 4 3

# ḣarper ⚜ ᴄorᴄḣbooḱs

## American Studies: General

HENRY STEELE COMMAGER, Ed.: The Struggle for Racial Equality TB/1300
CARL N. DEGLER: Out of Our Past: *The Forces that Shaped Modern America* CN/2
CARL N. DEGLER, Ed.: Pivotal Interpretations of American History
Vol. I TB/1240; Vol. II TB/1241
A. S. EISENSTADT, Ed.: The Craft of American History: *Selected Essays*
Vol. I TB/1255; Vol. II TB/1256
ROBERT L. HEILBRONER: The Limits of American Capitalism TB/1305
JOHN HIGHAM, Ed.: The Reconstruction of American History TB/1068
ROBERT H. JACKSON: The Supreme Court in the American System of Government TB/1106
JOHN F. KENNEDY: A Nation of immigrants. *Illus. Revised and Enlarged. Introduction by Robert F. Kennedy* TB/1118
RICHARD B. MORRIS: Fair Trial: *Fourteen Who Stood Accused, from Anne Hutchinson to Alger Hiss* TB/1335
GUNNAR MYRDAL: An American Dilemma: *The Negro Problem and Modern Democracy. Introduction by the Author.*
Vol. I TB/1443; Vol. II TB/1444
GILBERT OSOFSKY, Ed.: The Burden of Race: *A Documentary History of Negro-White Relations in America* TB/1405
ARNOLD ROSE: The Negro in America: *The Condensed Version of Gunnar Myrdal's An American Dilemma. Second Edition* TB/3048
JOHN E. SMITH: Themes in American Philosophy: *Purpose, Experience and Community* TB/1466
WILLIAM R. TAYLOR: Cavalier and Yankee: *The Old South and American National Character* TB/1474

## American Studies: Colonial

BERNARD BAILYN: The New England Merchants in the Seventeenth Century TB/1149
ROBERT E. BROWN: Middle-Class Democracy and Revolution in Massachusetts, 1691–1780. *New Introduction by Author* TB/1413
JOSEPH CHARLES: The Origins of the American Party System TB/1049
WESLEY FRANK CRAVEN: The Colonies in Transition: 1660-1712† TB/3084

CHARLES GIBSON: Spain in America † TB/3077
CHARLES GIBSON, Ed.: The Spanish Tradition in America + HR/1351
LAWRENCE HENRY GIPSON: The Coming of the Revolution: 1763-1775. † *Illus.* TB/3007
PERRY MILLER: Errand Into the Wilderness TB/1139
PERRY MILLER & T. H. JOHNSON, Eds.: The Puritans: *A Sourcebook of Their Writings*
Vol. I TB/1093; Vol. II TB/1094
EDMUND S. MORGAN: The Puritan Family: *Religion and Domestic Relations in Seventeenth Century New England* TB/1227
WALLACE NOTESTEIN: The English People on the Eve of Colonization: 1603-1630. † *Illus.* TB/3006
LOUIS B. WRIGHT: The Cultural Life of the American Colonies: 1607-1763. † *Illus.* TB/3005

## American Studies: The Revolution to 1860

JOHN R. ALDEN: The American Revolution: 1775-1783. † *Illus.* TB/3011
RAY A. BILLINGTON: The Far Western Frontier: 1830-1860. † *Illus.* TB/3012
GEORGE DANGERFIELD: The Awakening of American Nationalism, 1815-1828. † *Illus.* TB/3061
CLEMENT EATON: The Growth of Southern Civilization, 1790-1860. † *Illus.* TB/3040
LOUIS FILLER: The Crusade against Slavery: 1830-1860. † *Illus.* TB/3029
WILLIM W. FREEHLING: Prelude to Civil War: *The Nullification Controversy in South Carolina, 1816-1836* TB/1359
THOMAS JEFFERSON: Notes on the State of Virginia. ‡ *Edited by Thomas P. Abernethy* TB/3052
JOHN C. MILLER: The Federalist Era: 1789-1801. † *Illus.* TB/3027
RICHARD B. MORRIS: The American Revolution Reconsidered TB/1363
GILBERT OSOFSKY, Ed.: Puttin' On Ole Massa: *The Slave Narratives of Henry Bibb, William Wells Brown, and Solomon Northup* ‡ TB/1432
FRANCIS S. PHILBRICK: The Rise of the West, 1754-1830. † *Illus.* TB/3067
MARSHALL SMELSER: The Democratic Republic, 1801-1815 † TB/1406

---

† The New American Nation Series, edited by Henry Steele Commager and Richard B. Morris.
‡ American Perspectives series, edited by Bernard Wishy and William E. Leuchtenburg.
a History of Europe series, edited by J. H. Plumb.
§ The Library of Religion and Culture, edited by Benjamin Nelson.
‖ Researches in the Social, Cultural, and Behavioral Sciences, edited by Benjamin Nelson.
∥ Harper Modern Science Series, edited by James A. Newman.
° Not for sale in Canada.
+ Documentary History of the United States series, edited by Richard B. Morris.
# Documentary History of Western Civilization series, edited by Eugene C. Black and Leonard W. Levy.
ʌ The Economic History of the United States series, edited by Henry David et al.
¶ European Perspectives series, edited by Eugene C. Black.
** Contemporary Essays series, edited by Leonard W. Levy.
* The Stratum Series, edited by John Hale.

LOUIS B. WRIGHT: Culture on the Moving Frontier TB/1053

## American Studies: The Civil War to 1900

T. C. COCHRAN & WILLIAM MILLER: The Age of Enterprise: *A Social History of Industrial America* TB/1054
W. A. DUNNING: Reconstruction, Political and Economic: 1865-1877 TB/1073
HAROLD U. FAULKNER: Politics, Reform and Expansion: 1890-1900. † *Illus.* TB/3020
GEORGE M. FREDRICKSON: The Inner Civil War: *Northern Intellectuals and the Crisis of the Union* TB/1358
JOHN A. GARRATY: The New Commonwealth, 1877-1890 † TB/1410
HELEN HUNT JACKSON: A Century of Dishonor: *The Early Crusade for Indian Reform.* † *Edited by Andrew F. Rolle* TB/3063
WILLIAM G. MCLOUGHLIN, Ed.: The American Evangelicals, 1800-1900: An Anthology ‡ TB/1382
JAMES S. PIKE: The Prostrate State: *South Carolina under Negro Government.* ‡ *Intro. by Robert F. Durden* TB/3085
VERNON LANE WHARTON: The Negro in Mississippi, 1865-1890 TB/1178

## American Studies: The Twentieth Century

RAY STANNARD BAKER: Following the Color Line: *American Negro Citizenship in Progressive Era.* ‡ *Edited by Dewey W. Grantham, Jr. Illus.* TB/3053
RANDOLPH S. BOURNE: War and the Intellectuals: *Collected Essays, 1915-1919.* ‡ *Edited by Carl Resek* TB/3043
A. RUSSELL BUCHANAN: The United States and World War II. † *Illus.*
Vol. I TB/3044; Vol. II TB/3045
THOMAS C. COCHRAN: The American Business System: *A Historical Perspective, 1900-1955* TB/1080
FOSTER RHEA DULLES: America's Rise to World Power: 1898-1954. † *Illus.* TB/3021
HAROLD U. FAULKNER: The Decline of Laissez Faire, 1897-1917 TB/1397
JOHN D. HICKS: Republican Ascendancy: 1921-1933. † *Illus.* TB/3041
WILLIAM E. LEUCHTENBURG: Franklin D. Roosevelt and the New Deal: 1932-1940. † *Illus.* TB/3025
WILLIAM E. LEUCHTENBURG, Ed.: The New Deal: *A Documentary History* + HR/1354
ARTHUR S. LINK: Woodrow Wilson and the Progressive Era: 1910-1917. † *Illus.* TB/3023
BROADUS MITCHELL: Depression Decade: *From New Era through New Deal, 1929-1941* ∧ TB/1439
GEORGE E. MOWRY: The Era of Theodore Roosevelt and the Birth of Modern America: 1900-1912. † *Illus.* TB/3022
WILLIAM PRESTON, JR.: Aliens and Dissenters:
TWELVE SOUTHERNERS: I'll Take My Stand: *The South and the Agrarian Tradition. Intro. by Louis D. Rubin, Jr.; Biographical Essays by Virginia Rock* TB/1072

## Art, Art History, Aesthetics

ERWIN PANOFSKY: Renaissance and Renascences in Western Art. *Illus.* TB/1447
ERWIN PANOFSKY: Studies in Iconology: *Humanistic Themes in the Art of the Renaissance. 180 illus.* TB/1077
HEINRICH ZIMMER: Myths and Symbols in Indian Art and Civilization. *70 illus.* TB/2005

## Asian Studies

WOLFGANG FRANKE: China and the West: *The Cultural Encounter, 13th to 20th Centuries. Trans. by R. A. Wilson* TB/1326
L. CARRINGTON GOODRICH: A Short History of the Chinese People. *Illus.* TB/3015

## Economics & Economic History

C. E. BLACK: The Dynamics of Modernization: *A Study in Comparative History* TB/1321
GILBERT BURCK & EDITORS OF *Fortune:* The Computer Age: *And its Potential for Management* TB/1179
ROBERT L. HEILBRONER: The Future as History: *The Historic Currents of Our Time and the Direction in Which They Are Taking America* TB/1386
ROBERT L. HEILBRONER: The Great Ascent: *The Struggle for Economic Development in Our Time* TB/3030
FRANK H. KNIGHT: The Economic Organization TB/1214
DAVID S. LANDES: Bankers and Pashas: *International Finance and Economic Imperialism in Egypt. New Preface by the Author* TB/1412
ROBERT LATOUCHE: The Birth of Western Economy: *Economic Aspects of the Dark Ages* TB/1290
W. ARTHUR LEWIS: The Principles of Economic Planning. *New Introduction by the Author°* TB/1436
WILLIAM MILLER, Ed.: Men in Business: *Essays on the Historical Role of the Entrepreneur* TB/1081
HERBERT A. SIMON: The Shape of Automation: *For Men and Management* TB/1245

## Historiography and History of Ideas

J. BRONOWSKI & BRUCE MAZLISH: The Western Intellectual Tradition: *From Leonardo to Hegel* TB/3001
WILHELM DILTHEY: Pattern and Meaning in History: *Thoughts on History and Society.° Edited with an Intro. by H. P. Rickman* TB/1075
J. H. HEXTER: More's Utopia: *The Biography of an Idea. Epilogue by the Author* TB/1195
H. STUART HUGHES: History as Art and as Science: *Twin Vistas on the Past* TB/1207
ARTHUR O. LOVEJOY: The Great Chain of Being: *A Study of the History of an Idea* TB/1009
RICHARD H. POPKIN: The History of Scepticism from Erasmus to Descartes. *Revised Edition* TB/1391
BRUNO SNELL: The Discovery of the Mind: *The Greek Origins of European Thought* TB/1018

## History: General

HANS KOHN: The Age of Nationalism: *The First Era of Global History* TB/1380
BERNARD LEWIS: The Arabs in History TB/1029
BERNARD LEWIS: The Middle East and the West ° TB/1274

## History: Ancient

A. ANDREWS: The Greek Tyrants TB/1103
THEODOR H. GASTER: Thespis: *Ritual Myth and Drama in the Ancient Near East* TB/1281

A. H. M. JONES, Ed.: A History of Rome through the Fifth Century # *Vol. I: The Republic* HR/1364
*Vol. II The Empire:* HR/1460
SAMUEL NOAH KRAMER: Sumerian Mythology TB/1055
NAPHTALI LEWIS & MEYER REINHOLD, Eds.: Roman Civilization *Vol. I: The Republic* TB/1231
*Vol. II: The Empire* TB/1232

### History: Medieval

NORMAN COHN: The Pursuit of the Millennium: *Revolutionary Messianism in Medieval and Reformation Europe* TB/1037
F. L. GANSHOF: Feudalism TB/1058
F. L. GANSHOF: The Middle Ages: *A History of International Relations. Translated by Rémy Hall* TB/1411
HENRY CHARLES LEA: The Inquisition of the Middle Ages. || *Introduction by Walter Ullmann* TB/1456

### History: Renaissance & Reformation

JACOB BURCKHARDT: The Civilization of the Renaissance in Italy. *Introduction by Benjamin Nelson and Charles Trinkaus. Illus.* Vol. I TB/40; Vol. II TB/41
JOHN CALVIN & JACOPO SADOLETO: A Reformation Debate. *Edited by John C. Olin* TB/1239
J. H. ELLIOTT: Europe Divided, 1559-1598 *a* ° TB/1414
G. R. ELTON: Reformation Europe, 1517-1559 ° *a* TB/1270
HANS J. HILLERBRAND, Ed., The Protestant Reformation # HR/1342
JOHAN HUIZINGA: Erasmus and the Age of Reformation. *Illus.* TB/19
JOEL HURSTFIELD: The Elizabethan Nation TB/1312
JOEL HURSTFIELD, Ed.: The Reformation Crisis TB/1267
PAUL OSKAR KRISTELLER: Renaissance Thought: *The Classic, Scholastic, and Humanist Strains* TB/1048
DAVID LITTLE: Religion, Order and Law: *A Study in Pre-Revolutionary England. § Preface by R. Bellah* TB/1418
PAOLO ROSSI: Philosophy, Technology, and the Arts, in the Early Modern Era 1400-1700. || *Edited by Benjamin Nelson. Translated by Salvator Attanasio* TB/1458
H. R. TREVOR-ROPER: The European Witch-craze of the Sixteenth and Seventeenth Centuries and Other Essays ° TB/1416

### History: Modern European

ALAN BULLOCK: Hitler, A Study in Tyranny. ° *Revised Edition. Illus.* TB/1123
JOHANN GOTTLIEB FICHTE: Addresses to the German Nation. *Ed. with Intro. by George A. Kelly* ¶ TB/1366
ALBERT GOODWIN: The French Revolution TB/1064
STANLEY HOFFMANN et al.: In Search of France: *The Economy, Society and Political System In the Twentieth Century* TB/1219
H. STUART HUGHES: The Obstructed Path: *French Social Thought in the Years of Desperation* TB/1451
JOHAN HUIZINGA: Dutch Civilisation in the 17th Century and Other Essays TB/1453

JOHN MCMANNERS: European History, 1789-1914: *Men, Machines and Freedom* TB/1419
HUGH SETON-WATSON: Eastern Europe Between the Wars, 1918-1941 TB/1330
ALBERT SOREL: Europe Under the Old Regime. *Translated by Francis H. Herrick* TB/1121
A. J. P. TAYLOR: From Napoleon to Lenin: *Historical Essays* ° TB/1268
A. J. P. TAYLOR: The Habsburg Monarchy, 1809-1918: *A History of the Austrian Empire and Austria-Hungary* ° TB/1187
J. M. THOMPSON: European History, 1494-1789 TB/1431
H. R. TREVOR-ROPER: Historical Essays TB/1269

### Literature & Literary Criticism

W. J. BATE: From Classic to Romantic: *Premises of Taste in Eighteenth Century England* TB/1036
VAN WYCK BROOKS: Van Wyck Brooks: The Early Years: *A Selection from his Works, 1908-1921 Ed. with Intro. by Claire Sprague* TB/3082
RICHMOND LATTIMORE, Translator: The Odyssey of Homer TB/1389
ROBERT PREYER, Ed.: Victorian Literature ** TB/1302

### Philosophy

HENRI BERGSON: Time and Free Will: *An Essay on the Immediate Data of Consciousness* ° TB/1021
H. J. BLACKHAM: Six Existentialist Thinkers: *Kierkegaard, Nietzsche, Jaspers, Marcel, Heidegger, Sartre* ° TB/1002
J. M. BOCHENSKI: The Methods of Contemporary Thought. *Trans. by Peter Caws* TB/1377
ERNST CASSIRER: Rousseau, Kant and Goethe. *Intro. by Peter Gay* TB/1092
MICHAEL GELVEN: A Commentary on Heidegger's "Being and Time" TB/1464
J. GLENN GRAY: Hegel and Greek Thought TB/1409
W. K. C. GUTHRIE: The Greek Philosophers: *From Thales to Aristotle* ° TB/1008
G. W. F. HEGEL: Phenomenology of Mind. ° || *Introduction by George Lichtheim* TB/1303
MARTIN HEIDEGGER: Discourse on Thinking. *Translated with a Preface by John M. Anderson and E. Hans Freund. Introduction by John M. Anderson* TB/1459
F. H. HEINEMANN: Existentialism and the Modern Predicament TB/28
WERER HEISENBERG: Physics and Philosophy: *The Revolution in Modern Science. Intro. by F. S. C. Northrop* TB/549
EDMUND HUSSERL: Phenomenology and the Crisis of Philosophy. § *Translated with an Introduction by Quentin Lauer* TB/1170
IMMANUEL KANT: Groundwork of the Metaphysic of Morals. *Translated and Analyzed by H. J. Paton* TB/1159
WALTER KAUFMANN, Ed.: Religion From Tolstoy to Camus: *Basic Writings on Religious Truth and Morals* TB/123
QUENTIN LAUER: Phenomenology: *Its Genesis and Prospect. Preface by Aron Gurwitsch* TB/1169
MICHAEL POLANYI: Personal Knowledge: *Towards a Post-Critical Philosophy* TB/1158
WILLARD VAN ORMAN QUINE: Elementary Logic *Revised Edition* TB/577
WILHELM WINDELBAND: A History of Philosophy *Vol. I: Greek, Roman, Medieval* TB/38

3